CW01370851

FACING
JERUSALEM

God's Plan For Global Redemption

Printed with permission by HaYovel Inc.

Copyright © 2020 Luke Hilton & Zac Waller

ISBN: 9798684810817

All rights reserved. This book or parts thereof may not be reproduced in any form, stored in any retrieval system, or transmitted in any form by any means—electronic, mechanical, photocopy, recording, or otherwise—without prior written permission of the publisher, except as provided by United States of America copyright law. For permission requests, please contact: info@hayovel.com

Edited by: Jessica Sommerfield
Cover Design By: Havah Waller
Formatted By: Josiah Hilton

For comments or questions concerning the contents of this book, please feel free to contact the authors at: info@HaYovel.com

"Scripture taken from the New King James Version. Copyright © 1982 by Thomas Nelson, Inc. Used by permission. All rights reserved."

"Scripture quotations are from the ESV® Bible (The Holy Bible, English Standard Version®), copyright © 2001 by Crossway, a publishing ministry of Good News Publishers. Used by permission. All rights reserved."

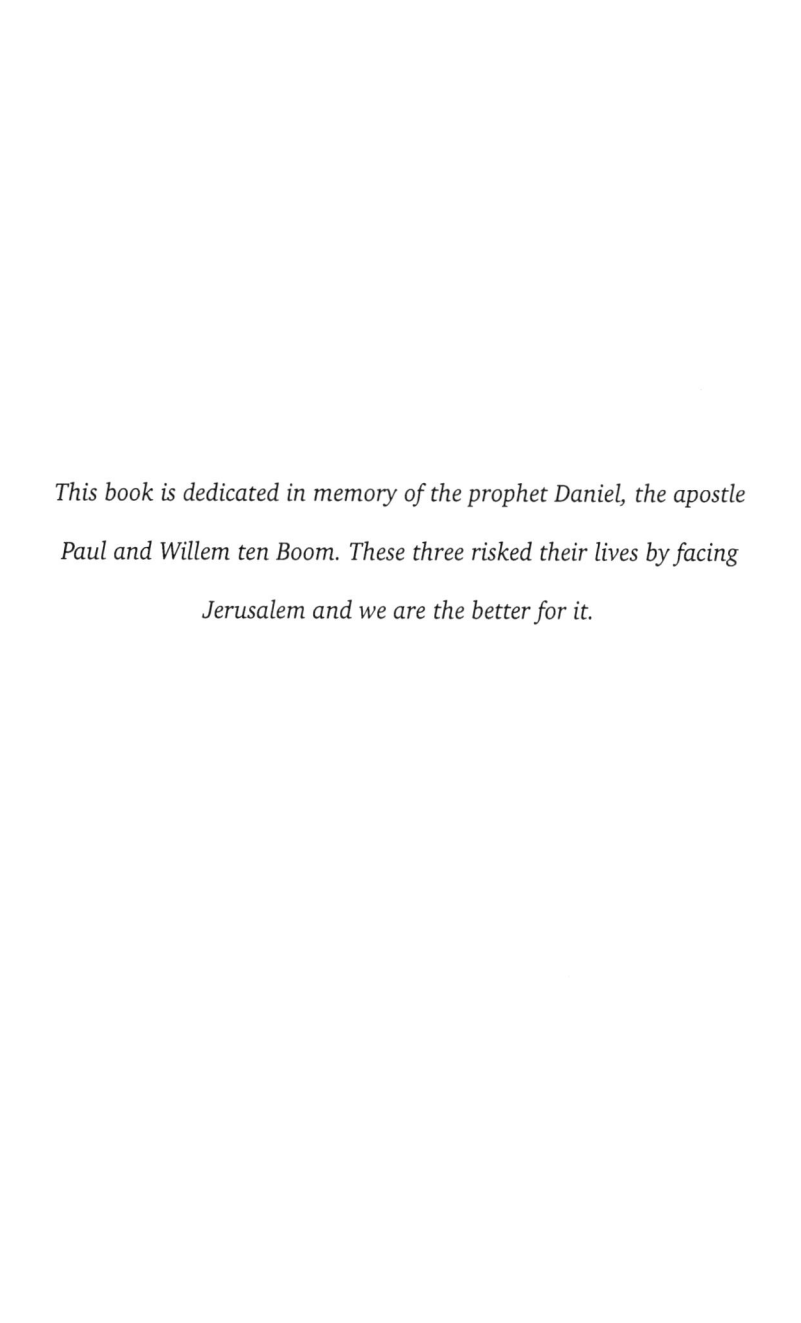

This book is dedicated in memory of the prophet Daniel, the apostle Paul and Willem ten Boom. These three risked their lives by facing Jerusalem and we are the better for it.

TABLE OF CONTENTS

Introduction -	I
Chapter 1 - The Prayer for the Foreigner	1
Chapter 2 - Where Is Christianity Today?	9
Chapter 3 - The Art of Rejecting the Truth	15
Chapter 4 - Separating from Jerusalem	21
Chapter 5 - The Sin of Rome	27
Chapter 6 - Turning Against the Jews	35
Chapter 7 - Dividing the Land of Israel	41
Chapter 8 - A Global Pandemic	49
Chapter 9 - Ancient Practices for a Modern Faith	55
Chapter 10 - Yeshua's Message: Repent!	59

Chapter 11 - Bypassing Rome	69
Chapter 12 - Returning to Our Roots	77
Chapter 13 - Christians in the Synagogues	83
Chapter 14 - Loving God's Chosen Place	93
Chapter 15 - Loving God's Word	103
Chapter 16 - Loving God's Chosen People	109
Chapter 17 - Modern Israel-Man's Creation or God's Hand?	121
Chapter 18 - Never Divide the Land of Israel	129
Chapter 19 - Lightly Esteeming Israel	135
Chapter 20 - The Sun & Moon Predictions	141
Chapter 21 - The Promise for the Foreigner	149
Chapter 22 - Time for Action	155
Acknowledgements	162

INTRODUCTION

Let's be honest. As Bible believers, most of us would say we support Israel. We probably all want to visit the holy land at least once in our lives. We consider ourselves very far removed from anti-semitism or replacement theology.

However, how far are we willing to take our love for Israel? Should it be all consuming to our faith and lives? Isn't it taking things a bit too far to allow Israel to be one of the main tenets of our faith?

Besides, there are a lot of really terrible things currently happening in the world. Even the US, long considered the superpower of the world, is experiencing major upheaval. Christians in other countries are experiencing horrific persecution. Millions of people are experiencing hunger, sickness, deprivation, and the basic provisions of normal life.

So even though we believe that Israel is important, aren't there other things that deserve our attention more than the holy land right now?

What if I told you that many of the disasters that have happened in the US over the last 70 years were directly related to America's treatment of Israel? What if I told you that every time the US Administration presented a plan that involved dividing the land of Israel, a natural disaster struck America within 24-48 hours?

What if the mass upheaval of 2020 in the US, including COVID-19 and the violence which swept across cities, are all connected to President Trump's "deal of the century" peace plan, one which calls for Israel to give away parts of its land?

When God first blessed Abraham in Genesis 12, he not only presented a covenant for the land and people of Israel, He initiated a plan for the salvation of the entire world. He told Abraham, "In you all families of the earth shall be blessed." ALL families of the earth would be BLESSED through ABRAHAM! Did you catch that? The blessings that we experience in our life are channeled through that original blessing that God gave to a man 4,000 years ago.

I'd like for you to change your glasses through which you've been viewing Israel and the Jewish people for a moment. Instead of seeing it as "us and them," think about it as a grand, master plan - a plan the Creator of the universe put together thousands of years ago to save a lost and broken world.

This book is not a deep theological work. Rather, it is a simple presentation from Zac Waller and myself of the incredible blessings to be experienced by aligning with the God, land, and people of Israel. By working in the land of Israel for the last fifteen years, we have experienced incredible physical and spiritual blessings from standing with God's promises for Israel. We want to share those blessings with you.

When Solomon dedicated the first temple, he asked God to answer the prayers of foreigners who prayed towards Jerusalem, even if they were in a far country. You might write that prayer off as not being valid today, but we would like to present a different narrative. In this book, we will go through Solomon's prayer as well as many other passages of Scripture to show that facing Jerusalem today is one of the most important actions that we can take in our Christian faith.

Instead of viewing it as one part of Christianity, or as a spiritual wand that we wave to lead us to prosperity, Israel should be a core principle of our faith. Following the prophets of old and the examples of Yeshua the Messiah Himself, facing Jerusalem and aligning ourselves with Zion is the catalyst that launches salvation to the rest of the world. Isaiah even prophesied that the law would go forth from Zion and God's word from Jerusalem. (Isaiah 2:3)

God's perfect plan of salvation for the world started with a blessing given to Abraham, on a hilltop in the land of Israel. It continued to be passed down from generation to generation, being validated time and time again. Yeshua our Messiah ultimately made the way for the rest of the world to become a part of God's perfect plan of salvation, and through Him, we have been given the opportunity to walk in this blessing.

This is what I believe to be God's master plan of redemption for the world.

Journey with us as we explore how facing Jerusalem is a pivotal part of our faith and crucial to physical and spiritual blessing in our lives. Could it be that this is God's key to initiating redemption for the entire world?

    Luke Hilton

Note: we'll be using the name "Yeshua" throughout this book, which is Aramaic/ Hebrew for "Jesus." To the best of our knowledge, this is the name that everyone who knew Him during His earthly ministry would have called Him, and we love to use the same name.

CHAPTER ONE

The Prayer for the Foreigner

Luke Hilton

Most religions have a central location of worship. Muslims have Mecca. Catholicism has the Vatican. Hindus look to Varanasi as their holy city.

I can vividly remember the first time I went to Jerusalem. As we drove through the newer neighborhoods of Jerusalem, I can remember my first glimpse of the Old City walls through the car window. I remember being surprised, although I'm not sure exactly why. Maybe it was because I wasn't prepared to see such massive, ancient walls set right in the midst of a thriving 21st-century city. Maybe it was the grandeur. I vividly remember being impressed.

Facing Jerusalem

After parking the car, we walked through Jaffa Gate and through the Christian Quarter, Armenian Quarter, and into the Jewish Quarter. We saw the Golden Menorah displayed close to the stairs that led down to the Western Wall plaza. I could hardly believe that a menorah so large was constructed entirely of gold, and was made in preparation for the building of the third temple!

My most vivid impression however, was when we walked up to the Western Wall to pray. I had never put a kippah on my head; however, if you're not wearing a hat, it is required for the men to wear one of the kippahs that are offered by a small stand as you enter the men's section. As I walked up to the ancient stones at the Wall, something came over me. An intense desire for God to restore His land and people. An intense desire to be a part of the restoration of God's Kingdom. I was only 16 at the time, and had no idea what that meant. In that moment when I touched the stones of the Western Wall for the first time however, I knew that I wanted to be a part of what God was doing in Israel. Now, every time that I visit the Western Wall or the Temple Mount, I pray a similar prayer, begging God to allow me to participate in the restoration of His Kingdom that will one day take place there.

Jerusalem is known as Israel's central place of worship today, but it wasn't always so. For years, the children of Israel wandered in the desert. Eventually, God revealed the laws of how His people were to worship Him and instructed Moses to set up a tabernacle. Even though the Israelites were wandering as a people, the tabernacle was a mobile temple of sorts. Wherever they went, the tabernacle was disassembled, carried with them, and set up at their next camping place.

After forty years of wandering in the desert, the children of Israel finally arrived in the Promised Land, and God helped them drive out their enemies. Finally, they had their own country to call home. You'd think that one of their first orders of business would be to set up the tabernacle in a permanent location or build a temple, a house for God. Well, for one reason or another, the tabernacle was set up in Shiloh as a temporary resting place. It stayed there for 369 years.

When David, who was undoubtedly one of Israel's greatest rulers, finally secured peace in Israel, he wanted to bring the ark of the covenant (the centerpiece of the tabernacle) up to Jerusalem. Unfortunately, he didn't follow the biblical instructions for transporting the ark, and catastrophe followed (2nd Samuel 6). Because of this, David put the ark of the covenant in a nearby home, where it remained for some time. Eventually, the Israelites figured out the proper way to transport the ark of the covenant, and David brought it up to Jerusalem with much rejoicing and fanfare before depositing it in a tent that was set up to house it. In David's heart, though, was a plan to build a beautiful temple, a place for the house of God.

God revealed to David, however, that he was not the man for the job. He had seen too much bloodshed during his reign as king. He was a man of war with blood on his hands. His son Solomon, however, would be the man to complete this momentous project. David decided to do everything in his power to prepare Solomon for the most important task of his life: building the Temple. He gathered the materials, stockpiled gold and silver, and wrote an instruction manual. After David died, Solomon finally built a house for the God of Abraham, Isaac and Jacob in the holy city of Jerusalem.

Solomon's Temple, also known as the First Temple, was historic, and subsequent temples in Jerusalem have failed to reach the same standards of beauty and excellence. When Nehemiah and Ezra led the people back to Jerusalem many years later and rebuilt the Temple, the people who had seen the beauty of Solomon's Temple wept when they realized how much they had lost when it was destroyed (Ezra 3:12).

After King David's preparation and gathering of materials, followed by years of building at the beginning of Solomon's reign, the time for the Temple's dedication had come. In a dramatic and emotional ceremony, Solomon dedicated the Temple as the house of God, a place for Israel to worship the

The Prayer for the Foreigner

God of Abraham, Isaac, and Jacob. After an emotional prayer for the people of Israel, an interesting thing happened—something unexpected. Solomon prayed for the foreigner. Foreigners? What would they be doing in Israel, much less Jerusalem, much less the Temple of the God of Abraham, Isaac, and Jacob?

This is what Solomon prayed:

"Moreover, concerning a foreigner, who *is* not of Your people Israel, but has come from a far country for Your name's sake (for they will hear of Your great name and Your strong hand and Your outstretched arm), when he comes and prays toward this temple, hear in heaven Your dwelling place, and do according to all for which the foreigner calls to You, that all peoples of the earth may know Your name and fear You, as *do* Your people Israel, and that they may know that this temple which I have built is called by Your name" (1 Kings 8:41-43).

As it turns out, foreigners have been making pilgrimages to Jerusalem throughout the centuries and millennia. From the Queen of Sheba to Charles Warren, dignitaries and common people have been attracted to this place of worship. Even during New Testament times, we read of foreigners coming to the Temple. Solomon even set up a special courtyard in the Temple where non-Jews could come and worship.

Facing Jerusalem

After the dedication of the Temple, God appeared to Solomon by night:

> Then the Lord appeared to Solomon by night, and said to him: "I have heard your prayer, and have chosen this place for Myself as a house of sacrifice. When I shut up heaven and there is no rain, or command the locusts to devour the land, or send pestilence among My people, if My people who are called by My name will humble themselves, and pray and seek My face, and turn from their wicked ways, then I will hear from heaven, and will forgive their sin and heal their land. Now My eyes will be open and My ears attentive to prayer made in this place. For now I have chosen and sanctified this house, that My name may be there forever; and My eyes and My heart will be there perpetually" (2 Chronicles 7:12-16).

You are probably familiar with this verse that talks about God's people humbling themselves, praying, and seeking His face. Most of us, however, are unfamiliar with the context. For starters, God is talking about the people of Israel. The land He is referring to is the land of Israel. Since Solomon included a special courtyard and a prayer for the foreigner, we can further conclude that there is a place for foreigners in this word from God, as well. The piece I believe many of us have missed, however, is the connection to Jerusalem.

Have we missed something in modern Christianity? Solomon spoke of a physical turning towards the Temple and a physical journey to Jerusalem. In spiritualizing so much of our faith, many of us have missed this part of the story.

Is this ancient prayer of Solomon's still relevant for us as Christians today?

Even more relevant for us is this question: were the first-century church and our Messiah connected to this ancient prayer of Solomon's?

These are the questions we will explore in the following chapters. Get ready to connect an ancient story of redemption to our modern faith.

CHAPTER TWO

Where Is Christianity Today?

Luke Hilton

I don't think any strong believer would argue the fact that the spiritual state of the world today is deplorable. In Western Christianity, the apathy that is so prevalent is causing Christians to leave the church and search for a religion that offers them structure, rules, guidelines—anything except a white-washed Christianity that tells them they can do anything they want.

I know of Christians who have left the church and converted to Mormonism simply because they found good morals there. The Mormon church offered their children a purpose and a vision to follow. It offered guidelines and rules they could give to their children.

I've heard of others who have left Protestantism for Catholicism. The reason? Very similar to that of Christians who converted to Mormonism: Catholicism offers rules. It sets boundaries and guidelines. In its own way, it offers a vision for those who want more than a faith that allows them to do whatever they want as long as they show up on Sunday.

Sin is rampant in Christianity today. Sins that the Bible specifically denounces are accepted under the guise that we just need to love everyone. That's true. Yeshua said we should love our fellow man as ourselves, but he never said we should love their sin! Whatever happened to the old adage "love the sinner but hate the sin"?

I was recently heartbroken to find out that a leader I had been regularly listening to was a Christian and an outspoken homosexual, even reconciling this lifestyle with the Bible. How does one reconcile a lifestyle that flies in the very face of what God created in the Garden of Eden?

Just in the last year, Christian media has reported numerous stories of drag queens being invited into the public libraries of the United States to lead story hours with the children. What has the state of our world come to? Are we too afraid to stand on the truth of God's Word anymore?

I recently spoke with some people who gushed that their church welcomed everyone. Whether they were gay, transvestite, or transgender, all were welcome. What's more, the church members were *particularly* welcoming to these people, seeming to endorse their lifestyle! Loving and welcoming people with these lifestyles is one thing, but what about telling them the truth of God's Word and how it directly opposes their choices? What example does seeming to endorse these people's lifestyles give to our children?

Many Christians tout the premise that the Old Testament, or at least its laws, have been done away with, and now we are to be led by the Spirit. At the same time, many are dissatisfied with the empty space that this leaves in their lives—to claim as their faith something that does not tell them what to do or what not to do. No rules. No guidelines. At the most, we cling to the Ten Commandments, but even some of those are in question or barely even followed.

Christians say they do not want to be tied to the laws that the Bible puts forth, but for the very same reason, many are leaving their faith.
The Gospel has been watered down to "you just need to love Yeshua, and everything will be okay." Instead of vision, Christians are touting love and acceptance.

I grew up in a very conservative Christian home, and I am extremely grateful to parents who instilled a concrete vision into me and my siblings. As we got older, we had a vision to latch onto that propelled us to grow in our faith, become leaders, and ultimately start our own families to pass that vision on to.

However, I've also noticed many people from my generation have fallen away from the principles their parents raised them with. The change from how their parents raised them to the worldly adventures they are now chasing is scary. Some still hold the pretense of Christianity, some are in the mainstream church, and some don't even bother calling themselves Christians anymore but have instead embraced a completely secular lifestyle.

I believe this all comes down to a lack of vision, or maybe their parents had a vision but failed to pass it on to their children.

Where there is no vision, the people perish (Proverbs 29:18). I have seen this statement ring true for many families I have seen change radically over the years. As believers, aren't we supposed to reflect the light of Yeshua? Aren't we supposed to be the light of the world? Aren't we supposed to have a vision for the restoration of God's Kingdom?

Where is Christianity Today?

I see little passion for God's Kingdom in today's world. How did we get to this place of looking, talking, and acting just like the world?

In much of the world, it is now normal to be a Christian and be okay with abortion.

Normal to be a Christian and be homosexual.

Normal to be a Christian and have no purity before marriage.

Normal to be a Christian and not believe that the entire Bible is the inspired and inerrant Word of God.

Normal to be a Christian and believe that the Ten Commandments are no longer relevant.

Normal to be a Christian and watch any movie you like.

Normal to be a Christian and welcome a transvestite into your church, failing to explain how God disagrees with their lifestyle.

What would it take for Christianity to become a living, breathing, thriving faith once again? What if we got back to the actual teachings of Yeshua and began living as faithful disciples of a Jewish Messiah?

I am grateful for the pastors, teachers, and leaders who are standing faithfully among the remnant of believers, calling them to a life of action, passion, and Bible-centered lifestyles. I am in no way placing all of Christianity or all churches in the category that I have described above. I know of many pastors who are still preaching a strong Gospel and casting a strong vision before their people. There are still many who are standing on God's Word as the basis for their faith walk.

Yes, the world has slipped into a very immoral state, even within Christianity. But there is still hope. Many are clinging to the faith of their forefathers, found in the teachings of a risen Messiah. These are the ones who refuse to have the word "tolerance" in their vocabulary when defining how they relate to the secular world.

CHAPTER THREE

The Art of Rejecting the Truth

Luke Hilton

I co-host a podcast each week with the slogan "Radical truth from Israel's front lines." I love this tagline because it is so incredibly clear and evokes not only truth but radical truth. I love that. So far, we have managed to hit on some pretty radical content, even when it doesn't tickle people's ears.

I'm not a theologian, pastor, or even someone with fancy degrees. That's why I'm always hesitant to make statements unless I know for sure they are founded in the Bible. Being based 100% on God's Word gives me the confidence to speak to the world things that are oftentimes difficult to take in and many times blatantly contradict what mainstream Christianity is teaching.

Facing Jerusalem

At some point in Western Christianity, we left the bandwagon of our Judeo-Christian heritage and began embracing Western, Greek, and Catholic tenants of faith. I'll share more on that later, but, basically, instead of getting our truth straight from the Bible, we took our beliefs and convictions from those who taught them to us from the pulpit.

Please don't get me wrong—I am a strong advocate for positioning yourself under spiritual authority and belonging to a congregation. I do not believe we are meant to isolate ourselves and only depend on our own interpretation of Scripture as the basis for our faith. However, we do need to be good Bereans (Acts 17:11). Examining the teachings of those we have placed ourselves under, we must make sure that our doctrine is rooted in God's Word. If the Bible does not clearly back it up, we should be extremely cautious about touting something as biblical truth.

The modern age of Western culture has scared Christians to the point that many do not want to proclaim absolute biblical truth for fear of offending someone who does not agree with them. Many times this reticence is rooted in the fear of losing their social status, being labeled a "radical," or even losing their job or position.

We want to please everyone in today's world. Social media has taken over our society to the extent that we often base our individual identities on how many likes, dislikes, shares, and comments we receive on our social media platforms.

Many churches are seeker-friendly and preach a prosperity doctrine just to attract more people. Come as you are. It doesn't matter where you are in life—we promise to love you. You can walk in blatant sin during the week and then come and worship God on Sunday. This is the watered-down message of the Gospel that many are hearing.

We have rejected the truth. When asked what the greatest commandment was, this is what our Messiah answered:

"Yeshua said to him, 'You shall love the Lord your God with all your heart, with all your soul, and with all your mind. This is the first and greatest commandment. And the second is like it: You shall love your neighbor as yourself. On these two commandments hang all the Law and the Prophets'" (Matthew 22:37-40).

I believe most Christians would align themselves with this statement. However, the definition of loving God with all of your heart, soul, and strength is ambiguous. Many people would say this means they need to show up at church on Sunday morning. Loving your neighbor might mean making sure to like their social media posts.

The conclusive definition of these two greatest commandments is in the Bible. However, most churches are not teaching this definition.
Can you truly love God and walk in blatant opposition to the teachings of the Bible?

(Again, I want to emphasize that there are still many churches that are standing valiantly with the truth of God. I am grateful to know of many organizations, ministries, churches, and leaders who are still taking a stand for radical Christianity today.)

Ecclesiastes says that there is nothing new under the sun. This is not a new state that we find ourselves in today. God sent a flood to destroy the earth during Noah's time because mankind had sunk to such depravity. God promised that He would never again destroy the world by a flood, but could He be gently trying to lead us back to Him through other means? Could natural disasters around the world be a signal from our Creator that He wants us to return to Him? We'll get into that later, but first, let's talk about the roots of our faith.

Christianity has made a massive shift in its 2,000-year history. Our faith has morphed into something that its founders never would have dreamed of during the first several hundred years of its existence. Could this drastic change have something to do with the state of Christianity today?

Let's go back to the beginning, to the time when Christianity separated from Jerusalem.

CHAPTER FOUR

Separating from Jerusalem

Luke Hilton

Even though Christianity has largely separated from Jerusalem as their spiritual and physical birthplace, the Mount of Olives still holds a special place for most Christians' faith. After all, it is the place from where Yeshua ascended into heaven and to where He will return!

The Jewish people also believe that the Messiah will arrive at the Mt of Olives when He makes His appearance. There is a popular joke that says when the Jews and Christians go to meet Him when He arrives they will ask, "is this your first or your second visit?"

Facing Jerusalem

My first visit to the Mt of Olives involved a camel. If you've ever visited, you have probably seen the same camel, or at least an animal from the same family business. On one of my more recent visits to the overlook on the Mt of Olives, I talked to the men who run the camel riding business. They told me that bringing camels to the Mt of Olives to offer rides to tourists had been in their family for more than 100 years! Now that's what I call a family business.

While I have not ridden the camel on the Mt of Olives since my first visit, it was definitely worth that first experience. Perched on top of such a huge creature was exhilarating and gave me an even better view of the Old City and the valley below. Little did I know that similar to the shaking and bumping of that first camel ride, Jerusalem would become an issue that has shaken the theology of not only my faith, but the faith of millions of Christians worldwide.

In much of Christianity, Jerusalem is viewed as only a spiritual place or as a synonym for Heaven. New Jerusalem is often cited as another name for where we're all going when we are raptured out of this world at the end of days. Yet, these doctrines were rocked when Israel was re-founded as a nation in 1948 and again when Jerusalem was liberated in 1967. Now, what was Christianity to do? We now have a literal, physical place called Jerusalem!

Separating from Jerusalem

Maybe we should look at the early church for clarity. Did the early disciples and apostles ever mean to disconnect from the holy city in the land of promise? How did they relate to Jerusalem?

After Yeshua died, the disciples hid in a locked room in Jerusalem, fearful of repercussions from the authorities. After the Messiah rose again, they went back to Galilee for a time before returning to Jerusalem, where they ultimately witnessed the ascension of Yeshua.

After delivering his final commission to the disciples on the Mount of Olives, Yeshua ascended into Heaven. While the disciples were still gazing into the sky, two angels appeared and told them that, one day, they could expect to see the Messiah reappear in the same way that he left them. Zechariah 14:4 verifies this:

"And in that day His feet will stand on the Mount of Olives, which faces Jerusalem on the east, and the Mount of Olives shall be split in two, from east to west, making a very large valley; Half of the mountain shall move toward the north and half of it toward the south."

The Gospel of Luke records the following just after Yeshua ascended from the Mount of Olives:

"And they worshiped Him, and returned to Jerusalem with great joy, and were continually in the Temple praising and blessing God. Amen" (Luke 24:52-53).

Did you catch that? They returned to Jerusalem and were continually in the Temple, praising and blessing God! They were a part of the regular Jewish worship that was happening in the Temple in Jerusalem on a daily basis!

When I go to the Mt of Olives today, I like to imagine what it was like during the times of the Gospels. How did the area look back then? Was the terrain on the hillside and valley leading to the Temple area different 2,000 years ago, aside from the several thousand graves that today dot the area? I've done the hike from the old city to the Mt of Olives (and vice-versa) multiple times, and I've wondered if it was a similar route that Yeshua and His disciples took. Yeshua often spent His nights in Bethany, and traveled to the temple during the day, and so would have walked a very similar path! It's just sad that we can no longer travel straight into the Temple Mount area using the Eastern Gate, as it has long been closed off to anyone's entrance. It's very possible that the next entrance through this gate will be by Yeshua Himself, even though there will be some concrete to get rid of first. Something tells me it won't be a problem for the Messiah though.

Other places in the Gospels record our Master weeping over Jerusalem when he foresaw its coming destruction. Yeshua loved Jerusalem! That much is clear by how much time He spent in the holy city and the Temple courts and the time He was left behind for three days in the Temple when He was only twelve. We read that once when journeying towards Jerusalem, He steadfastly set his face towards that city (see Luke 9:53).

The early history of the church gets complex in regards to the separation from Jerusalem over the first several centuries. Before the Gospel was preached to the Gentiles, it was clear. The early believers were known as a sect of Judaism, and they operated as such. After a time, however, the ruling Jewish leaders of the day began to regard the believers as heretics, and they were eventually banned from worshipping in the synagogues. Also early on, the Gospel was preached to the Gentiles, and very quickly the question arose: should Gentile believers convert to Judaism (as this was the only practice the Jewish believers knew) or remain Gentiles and cling to their faith in Yeshua?

After much debate, the church in Jerusalem made a famous decision that we find outlined in Acts 15. Gentile believers should adhere to four basic principles of Judaism and, from there, should listen to the books of Moses (Genesis to Deuteronomy) being read in the synagogues every week.

"For Moses has had throughout many generations those who preach him in every city, being read in the synagogues every Sabbath" (Acts 15:21).

It is very clear from this passage that the elders in Jerusalem expected the Gentile believers to learn about Judaism and the Jewish roots of their faith. However, they did not expect a full conversion to Judaism.

After several centuries, as the Gospel began to spread far and wide, the gaps between Judaism and Christianity widened. Later, when Constantine declared himself to be a Christian and legalized Christianity in the Western world, he further widened the gap by banning all things Jewish amongst the believers. He switched the Sabbath worship that so many were used to keeping on the seventh day to the first day of the week. He even went so far as to make it illegal to worship on the seventh day.

From this point, a faith that began in Jerusalem continued to drift further and further away from its roots, eventually making its headquarters in an empire that was responsible for destroying Jerusalem: Rome.

The place known to us today as the birthplace of Christianity was the headquarters of an empire ultimately responsible for destroying the actual place where Christianity was born.

CHAPTER FIVE

The Sin of Rome

Luke Hilton

Being based here in Israel most of every year, we take the opportunity to ascend the Temple Mount in Jerusalem as often as we can. This year, when Rabbi Yehuda Glick extended an invitation to ascend the Mount on the Ninth of Av, we quickly made plans to join him. (The Ninth of Av is a biblical fast day which is commemorated annually to mourn the destruction of the first and second temples in Jerusalem.)

I rose early and dressed, skipping breakfast so that I could join the fast in unity with our Jewish brothers. I woke my three-year-old son, and together we loaded into the vehicles with the rest of the team and headed to Jerusalem. As we drove, I pondered what I wanted to experience while on the Temple Mount this year. Normally while there, I pray that the Temple would be rebuilt, that Israel would be restored, and that the Messiah would come. Today however, I knew we were commemorating the tragedy of the temple being destroyed. This day is specifically set aside to mourn the destruction of God's house. I decided that I wanted to really imagine what that was like.

We arrived at the entrance of the Temple Mount about a half hour before we were scheduled to go up. I was somewhat surprised to see several hundred Jewish people lined up at the entrance, waiting for the gate to open. Several years ago, the Temple Mount was not even open on the Ninth of Av! After our group entered the plaza area, we had to wait for a few moments while our police escort was assembled. While we waited, several other police officers passed us, leading four Jews toward the exit. It was clear that they were being expelled from the Temple Mount for doing something that was not allowed. I found out later that their "crime" was prostrating themselves in prayer. They simply laid down on the ground facing the direction of the Holy of Holies and were immediately arrested and removed from the site.

As we began our walk around the plaza, surrounded by a group of Israeli policemen, I began to imagine what the Temple Mount would have looked like two thousand years ago. Instead of border police officers guarding our group from Muslim extremists, there would have been Jewish zealots, guarding the

Temple courtyard from the attacks of the Romans. Instead of the Dome of the Rock and the Al Aqsa mosque with its worshippers praying to Allah, there would have been a beautiful temple, inviting pilgrims to worship the God of Abraham, Isaac, and Jacob.

As we rounded the plaza, several of the Jews in our group openly prayed and spoke to our group about the importance of the day. One of the more passionate men burst into tears at several points during our visit, visibly moved as he gazed and prayed toward the spot where the temple should be. I even heard another group loudly praying the "Shema Israel" prayer in unison! The police were very gracious in allowing prayer, songs, and teaching throughout the visit.

As we paused at our last stop before being politely escorted to the exit, I gazed at the Dome of the Rock while standing beside my three-year-old son. I tried to imagine what that day must have been like when the Romans finally broke into the Temple courtyard. I pictured Roman soldiers chasing down Jewish zealots and slaughtering them mercilessly. One of the soldiers hurled a blazing torch through an opening in the temple. When the Roman commander Titus saw the beauty of the place, he tried to stop the blaze, but it was too late.

The temple was burned and the Romans dismantled the structure until there was not one stone left upon another.

Why do we look to Rome as the center of our faith? Many of you are probably thinking, "We don't look to Rome as the center of our faith; that's only for Catholics." That may be true, but when Christianity completely separated from Judaism, its new capital was Rome, and it was many centuries before Protestantism was born. Whether we like it or not, Rome has had a massive influence on the Christianity we know today and remains responsible for many of its basic tenets. The influence that it has had on our faith is much greater than most of us realize.

The most devastating incident in Jewish history—and, I can confidently say, Christian history at the time—was the destruction of the Temple and the city of Jerusalem in 70 AD. At the time, Christianity was still very much a part of Judaism, and the early disciples had no reason not to be intrinsically connected to the place that Yeshua loved so much. The Temple that Yeshua said should have been a house of prayer for all nations was burned to the ground. The place that Yeshua wept over was completely destroyed only a short time after His death and resurrection.

The Romans had no regard for the sanctity of Jerusalem. By the time they conquered the city, the Roman soldiers were so enraged at the obstinacy of the Jewish zealots they were fighting that they torched the holy courts of the Temple.

The Sin of Rome

Ultimately, the Romans wanted to be the superpower of their day. Any people or nation who opposed them were trodden underfoot. Anything they wanted from the nations they conquered they took for themselves. They ravaged lands and carried away the people into slavery.

An example of this is how they treated the Judean vineyards. Today, there are more than 300 wine and olive presses located throughout Judea and Samaria that date back to the times of the Temple. (Judea and Samaria are the regions located just north and south of Jerusalem. During the time of the second Temple, the entire area was known as Judea.) Just from looking at these ancient presses, one can easily conclude that wine and olive oil were produced here. One can further conclude that the wine and olive oil that came from these regions were of the highest quality. How do we know? Wine and olive oil were used in the offerings in the Temple, and we know that the Jewish people always brought their best to offer to God.

A legend says that when the Romans conquered Jerusalem in 70 AD, they uprooted vines from Israel and took them to Rome. Today, the areas around the world that are most famous for their wines are—you guessed it—Italy, France, and the surrounding areas in Europe. On a side note, these same vineyards have been reestablished in Israel, just as the prophet Jeremiah foretold (Jer. 31:5). The regions of Judea and Samaria are becoming famous for their wine production once again.

Facing Jerusalem

After years of occupying and oppressing the Jewish people, Rome put the nail in the coffin by ravaging the land, brutally killing the people, and completely destroying Jerusalem and the holy Temple. From 70 AD on, the Jewish people were scattered to the four corners of the earth and did not gather again as one people until 1948 when Israel was re-established as a nation. If Rome was responsible for destroying Israel, the Jewish people, and the roots of early Christianity, why does Rome remain the capital of foundational Christianity today?

I already spoke about how Constantine deliberately steered Christianity away from its Jewish roots. The Catholic Church even openly admits its responsibility for officially changing the Sabbath from the seventh day to the first day of the week.

Christianity started as a sect of Judaism. In keeping with their Master Yeshua, the early disciples practiced their faith in the Temple in Jerusalem, and when they were not there, they worshipped in the synagogues in whatever city they found themselves in. However, as part of the fallout when Rome destroyed Israel, Christianity separated from its foundation. Our faith left its roots and the early teachings of our Master and put down new roots in the very place responsible for destroying the original roots. Our Master wept and cried over Jerusalem's coming destruction, yet we now look to the destroyers of Jerusalem as the architects of our faith.

The Sin of Rome

I realize that many of us would not align ourselves with Catholicism or view Rome as the capital of Christianity. Yet, it is entrenched in the roots of our faith more than we realize. Whether we like it or not, the very destroyers of Judaism and the early roots of Christianity are firmly embedded in our history. It's not the only thing that plagues the shadows of our faith though. Jew hatred was taught and encouraged by a man who is considered the father of the Christian reformation.

CHAPTER SIX

Turning Against the Jews

Luke Hilton

We've already seen how the gap between Judaism and Christianity began and slowly widened over the early years of our faith until it reached total division. Yet history does not stop there. Not only did Christianity split completely from Judaism, but it also reached a place of total disgust and hatred in the eyes of Judaism, and—unfortunately—rightly so.

Early crusades to conquer Jerusalem were not pretty when it comes to their treatment of the Jews. So-called Christians who were zealous to liberate the holy city and reclaim it for the name of Christ did not consider the very ones who would be considered Messiah's brethren. "Kiss the cross or die" many times was the mantra that was placed before the Jews when the conquering Christians came to their doorstep. Many chose to die rather than embrace the cross of Christianity.

Pogroms, the expelling of Jews from their home countries, and the Spanish Inquisition all place dark stains on Christianity's history.

Christians falsely accused the Jews of blood libels and horrendous things that can hardly even be spoken of, yet they were believed by the masses. As the saying goes, "if you speak a lie long enough and loud enough, it will begin to be believed."

Martin Luther, known widely as the father of the Protestant Reformation, at first tried to evangelize the Jews. When he made no progress, he then reversed his position and violently advocated for their persecution, subjugation, and even murder. In his book *Of the Jews and Their Lies*, he says:

"I had made up my mind to write no more either about the Jews or against them. But since I learned that these miserable and accursed people do not cease to lure to themselves even us, that is, the Christians, I have published this little book, so that I might be found among those who opposed such poisonous activities of the Jews who warned the Christians to be on their guard against them. I would not have believed that a Christian could be duped by the Jews into taking their exile and wretchedness upon himself. However, the devil is the god of the world, and wherever God's word is absent he has an easy task, not only with the weak but also with the strong. May God help us. Amen.

Therefore the blind Jews are truly stupid fools…

Therefore be on your guard against the Jews, knowing that wherever they have their synagogues, nothing is found but a den of devils in which sheer self glory, conceit, lies, blasphemy, and defaming of God and men are practiced most maliciously and veheming his eyes on them.

First, that their synagogues be burned down, and that all who are able toss in sulphur and pitch; it would be good if someone could also throw in some hellfire. That would demonstrate to God our serious resolve and be evidence to all the world that it was in ignorance that we tolerated such houses, in which the Jews have reviled God, our dear Creator and Father, and his Son most shamefully up till now but that we have now given them their due reward."

The extent of the persecution and killing of Jews throughout the last two thousand years is difficult to fathom and often rejected by believers today. However, all of this persecution pales in comparison to the Holocaust, which killed six million Jewish

Footnote: "Anti-Semitism: Martin Luther - the Jews and Their Lies (1543)," Jewish Virtual Library, accessed July 2020, *https://www.jewishvirtuallibrary.org/martin-luther-quot-the-jews-and-their-lies-quot*.

men, women, and children. To make it even more horrific, the mass murder of Jews during World War II was done in the very name of Christ.

You may be thinking, "Adolf Hitler was *not* a Christian!" or "There is no way that the Holocaust was committed in the name of Christianity!" While I definitely do not believe that Hitler was a Christian, he confessed Yeshua as his LORD and Savior, and he was never excommunicated from the Catholic Church.

To justify his actions, Hitler even quoted from Martin Luther's teachings about the Jews! While many of the Nazi death camps operated throughout the week with their killing machines, on Sundays, they often closed so that Nazi soldiers and their families could attend church.

These things are difficult to acknowledge. You might believe that history has nothing to do with you. Of course, none of us would claim that Adolf Hitler was actually a Christian or that any of his actions were justified by the Bible or Christian beliefs. However, the Holocaust left a terrible stain on the name of Yeshua. As our Messiah's disciples, we have the opportunity to take up the mantle of repenting for this horrific sin.

Today, most Jewish people are very aware of this stain on Christianity's history and would attribute the Holocaust to Christians. Even if you define yourself as a Protestant, Messianic, or Hebrew Roots Christian, it makes no difference to Jews. To them, Christianity is all in one box, including Catholicism and evangelical denominations.

If we truly want to make a difference and move on, we must start with repenting to our Jewish brothers and sisters for the awful stain that our forefathers placed on the name of Messiah. It is no wonder that our two faiths have been driven so far apart.

Over the last 2,000 years, a faith that was born in Jerusalem slowly drifted westward and, today, could not be farther from Jerusalem than ever. Now that Israel has been reborn, however, modern Christianity can no longer deny that a physical land and people not only survived history but are thriving in Israel today.

How has Christianity treated the modern state of Israel? Often, not according to our biblical mandate.

CHAPTER SEVEN

Dividing the Land of Israel

Luke Hilton

Israel became a nation in 1948 after 2,000 years of exile and dispersion. No one thought it was humanly possible, and indeed, it had never been done before in history. Never had there been a nation that once existed, was brutally destroyed and its people dispersed, then many years later was established on the same land, with its original language revived and its own people returned. There is only one word to describe the phenomenon: miraculous.

However, when the dust settled after the war of 1948, the borders that were drawn left Israel with only part of its God-given land. The Golan Heights, Sinai Peninsula, Gaza Strip, and East Jerusalem, Judea, and Samaria all remained in enemy hands. Ironically, these places are the most significant in terms of their historical and biblical connections. All of the covenants that were ratified with Abraham, Isaac, and Jacob happened in these places. All of the recorded land purchases in the Bible were in these territories. More than eighty percent of our Bible was written or took place here. That is why today, these areas of real estate are affectionately called in Hebrew "*Lev Haaretz*," or "Heartland."

After nineteen years of occupation, Israel went to war in self-defense in 1967. When the dust settled once again, Israel had liberated all of its Heartland—the Golan Heights, Sinai Peninsula, Gaza Strip, Jerusalem, Judea, and Samaria. If you follow the news today, you'll often hear negative references to Israel's occupation of "Palestine" and the use of terms such as "West Bank," "occupied territories," etc. These terms refer to East Jerusalem, Judea and Samaria, and sometimes the Golan Heights. The rest of the areas Israel has given up to its Arab neighbors in a desperate search for peace—a peace which, despite Israel's great sacrifices, has still remained elusive. Since the war of 1967, Israel has given up more than ninety percent of the original territory it regained, all in the name of peace.

If it had been up to various Israeli and world leaders, Israel would have relinquished even more land. Fortunately for Israel, more times than not, those with whom Israel offered to negotiate rejected its offers of land for peace. If you move past

Dividing the Land of Israel

all of the mainstream international media and look at the facts on the ground, you'll find that many Arab nations and the Palestinian people do not want the Heartland—or any other piece of land in Israel—as their home. They want the entire country of Israel, and they want its people (the Jews) pushed into the sea. In other words, they want the total annihilation of Israel and the entire holy land for themselves.

If we are biblical, Zionist Christians, we need to pay attention to Scripture when it comes to the land of Israel.

"For behold, in those days and at that time, when I bring back the captives of Judah and Jerusalem, I will also gather all nations, and bring them down to the Valley of Jehoshaphat; and I will enter into judgment with them there on account of My people, My heritage Israel, whom they have scattered among the nations; they have also divided up My land" (Joel 3:1-3).

It's pretty clear that God does not have very good plans for those who try to divide up His land. It is also very clear that He has brought back the captives of Judah and Jerusalem to their homes. We are living in the times of the restoration of Israel! If God is so clear about how He feels about dividing up His land, we should also be clear about our position on the same issue.

Scripture is not the only source that tells us what will happen to those who try to divide the land of Israel. Ancient and modern history have exactly matched God's feelings on the subject. A popular t-shirt that sells in the tourist shops in Israel lists all of the nations that have tried to destroy the Jewish people over the millennia. Then it lists their current status today:

- Ancient Egypt: gone

- The Philistines: gone

- Assyrian Empire: gone

- Babylonian Empire: gone

- Persian Empire: gone

- Nazi Germany: gone

The list goes on and on. Recent history also records what has happened to countries whose leaders have tried to force Israel to divide its land in exchange for the promise of peace. The following is an excerpt from "Don't Touch the Apple of God's Eye," an article my brother Ben Hilton wrote for the *Israel Heartland Report*, a weekly newsletter with a focus on Israel's Heartland:

"For several years now President Donald Trump and his team have been working on an Israeli Palestinian peace plan that involves **the creation of a Palestinian State in major portions of Judea and Samaria.** President Trump chose to release the details of his plan on **January 28th, 2020.** Many countries around the world responded to this plan with either their support or by expressing their commitment to the idea of a Palestinian State in all of Judea and Samaria. Among these countries were China, Iran, and the European Union.

On January 30th, just two days after Trump made his official announcement about the Deal of the Century, the World Health Organization officially declared the CoronaVirus as a global health emergency. I would be tempted to write this off as a mere coincidence, a random meeting of circumstances, and it may be. But, could it be possible that this might be God's answer to the proposal of dividing His land? Whether it is or not, there does seem to be a compelling pattern throughout our history to this effect. Take these few incidents for example:

On March 26th, 1979, Jimmy Carter facilitated a peace treaty between the nations of Israel and Egypt. Details of the treaty involved Israel giving up the entire Sinai Peninsula to Egypt, evacuating several Israeli communities in the process. Two days later on March 28th, Dauphin County Pennsylvania experienced a partial meltdown of one of their nuclear reactors, resulting in significant radiation leaks. The incident was so severe, it was awarded a five-point out of seven rating on the international nuclear event scale.

Facing Jerusalem

On October 20th, 1991, Geoge H. Bush facilitated an international conference for Middle East peace. Ten days later, what became known as the "Perfect Storm," a hurricane, struck the North American coastline from Canada all the way down to Puerto Rico. 38,000 people were left without power and damages from the storm [amounted] to over 200 million dollars.

On August 23rd, 1992, George H. Bush moved the peace talks to Washington for four days, setting the framework for the Oslo Accords, an agreement that awarded Palestinian sovereignty to large swaths of land in Judea and Samaria. **The very next day Hurricane Andrew made landfall on the coast of Florida** damaging 63,000 homes and causing 23 billion dollars worth of damages.

On January 16th, 1994, President Bill Clinton held talks with President Assad of Syria about a peace agreement with Israel that would involve Israel giving up possession of the Golan Heights. **The very next day a 6.7 magnitude earthquake struck the San Fernando Valley in California.** The earthquake became the largest earthquake ever to be recorded in an urban area in North America and caused 35 billion dollars worth of damages.

In September 1998, the Clinton Administration was once again in the process of drafting a plan for a Palestinian state, only this one would involve Israel surrendering 13% of Judea, Samaria, and Gaza. Shortly afterwards in mid-September, Hurricane George struck America's southern border causing over 14 billion dollars worth of damages.

On April 23rd, 2003, the George W. Bush administration released a document called the Roadmap to Peace. Once again this document was aimed at the establishment of a Palestinian State. The very same day the document was released, tornados began forming over several states. **Over the course of the next two weeks, states across America were hit with over 400 consecutive tornados,** causing over millions of dollars in damages.

In 2005, the Israeli government decided to remove all Jewish settlers out of Gaza and several communities in Northern Samaria. This was done with the strong support of the Bush administration. The deadline for the settlers to be out of their homes was August 15th. **Ten days later, Hurricane Katrina made landfall in Florida** destroying 800,000 homes and causing 125 billion dollars in damages.

On May 19th, 2011, Barack Obama officially called on the Israeli government to create a Palestinian State and return to pre-1967 borders. Three days later, Missouri was hit with the deadliest tornado ever recorded in U.S. history, costing nearly 3 billion dollars in damages."

Footnote: Hilton, Ben, "Don't Touch the Apple of God's Eye," *Israel Heartland Report*, March 20, 2020, https://www.israelheartlandreport.com/news/dont-touch-the-apple-of-gods-eye.

We'll have more on the Trump Peace Plan, otherwise known as the "deal of the century," which at the time of this writing, is in the process of potentially being implemented in Israel. Also at the time of this writing, the world is in a global pandemic, the likes of which has not been seen in nearly one hundred years. Coincidence? We'll explore more in the next chapter.

CHAPTER EIGHT

A Global Pandemic

Luke Hilton

At the time of this writing, there is a pandemic sweeping the entire world. It's called COVID-19, a virus that has essentially shut down nearly every economy and country in the world. Whatever your opinion of the virus, the outcome is hard to dispute.

There are plenty of conspiracy theories and speculations going around the internet about what this pandemic is. Some say it's a conspiracy by the US government to take the world into a New World Order. Some say this is the government's excuse for forcing American citizens to stay in their homes and taking away their freedoms.

Others say the virus was intentionally released by China and hidden for months until the world was infected.

Others, those probably closest to the truth in my own opinion, say that this is simply a nasty virus, similar to the flu, that has a high rate of contagion. The elderly and those with pre-existing medical conditions, especially respiratory problems, are at the greatest risk. Given time and proper response from world leaders, this virus will either go away, perhaps revisiting the world from time to time, or simply fade into the annals of history. It might even be around to stay, and we'll simply have to learn to live with it as we have with the flu.

The question is, where did this virus come from and why did it attack so much of the world? While I believe that diseases are part of the natural processes of our fallen human world, I also believe that God uses natural disasters to get our attention.

We've already discussed how history has shown that, when world leaders have tried to divide the land of Israel, natural disasters followed almost immediately. You might ask, "Who is currently trying to divide the land of Israel?" While many world leaders, Christian and secular alike, have lauded the praises of President Trump's "deal of the century," there is a definite part of the plan that seeks to divide the Holy Land.

A Global Pandemic

The reason so many leaders are in favor of President Trump's Middle East peace plan is that it calls for partial Israeli sovereignty in Judea and Samaria, something which has never been presented in previous peace plans over the years (and there have been a lot!). President Trump courageously decided to forgo all of his predecessors' plans that sought to bring peace to the region and boldly detailed a plan that calls for Israeli sovereignty over thirty percent of the West Bank.

Wait. Sovereignty will be applied over only thirty percent of Israel's Heartland? What about the rest? Yes, the rest will be established as a Palestinian state, or so the plan calls for. Although declared sovereign, fifteen of the Jewish settlements will remain as isolated enclaves in the midst of a Palestinian state. They will only have one-road access to Israel's main regions, roads that will pass through the Palestinian state. If history serves to repeat itself, this new Palestinian state will not be friendly to Israel, to put it mildly. Based on what the Gaza Strip has become and the current attitude of the Palestinians, their new state will be a full-fledged terrorist entity.

While bringing some amazing things to the table for Israel, the "deal of the century" still seeks to divide the land that God promised to Abraham, Isaac, Jacob, and their descendants forever. And not only that—it also seeks to give away the very part of the land that is rightly named the "Biblical Heartland." As

I've said before, more than eighty percent of our Bible was written or occurred here!

Dividing the land of Israel in any way, shape, or form is simply not right. It goes directly against Scripture (Joel 3). It seeks to make null and void a covenant that God said in His Word will continue forever (Psalms 105:8-11).

Back to COVID-19. President Trump revealed the "deal of the century" on January 28th, 2020. Two days later, the World Health Organization officially declared the novel coronavirus to be a global health emergency. To date, the United States has been the hardest-hit country in the world.

Are COVID-19 and a peace plan that seeks to divide Israel connected? If there is any doubt in your mind, just read Joel 3 again. Let me emphasize that I do believe that natural disasters are, well, natural. At the same time, I believe that God has a master plan that was put in place before the creation of the world, and when natural disasters occur, we should take the opportunity to look up and ask Him what He is trying to tell us. We should find out where we may have slipped in our walk, individually and nationally, and repent and turn back to Him.

Is there a connection between countries that have been hit the hardest by the coronavirus and God's Word? I can definitely think of a few:

- The United States put out a plan to divide the land of Israel two days before COVID-19 was declared a global emergency. To date, it has seen the most deaths from the virus.

- Iran is arguably the greatest enemy of all things Judeo-Christian. Its leaders call Israel "Little Satan" and America "Big Satan" and regularly call for the destruction of both countries.

- COVID-19 started in China, which is near the top of the list of countries that have felt the disease the worst. It is no secret that terrible persecution of the Christian faith takes place in this Communist country.

- Italy has also been hit extremely hard with COVID-19. I didn't understand the spiritual connection to this country until someone pointed out to me that Italy represents ancient Rome and is the seat of the Vatican. Rome was also guilty of destroying Jerusalem and scattering the Jewish people to the diaspora for 2,000 years.

We could go on, but I'll stop there. The point is, God wants to get our attention. We don't want to miss his warning signs.

CHAPTER NINE

Ancient Practices for a Modern Faith

Luke Hilton

We've spent the first part of this book discussing the problems the world is facing today and how they may be connected to our faith. Hold on tight because we're about to get into a solution that I believe is firmly rooted in the Bible and the ancient practices of our faith.

Earlier in this book, we told the story of Solomon building and dedicating the Temple in Jerusalem. He finished with a prayer to God asking that when foreigners (those from outside Israel) prayed towards Jerusalem, God would hear and answer their prayers. God appeared to Solomon that night, affirming that his prayers were heard.

Facing Jerusalem

You might think that praying towards Jerusalem is just an ancient practice and not employed by anyone today. After all, the Temple was destroyed. You may or may not be surprised that the Jewish people still pray towards Jerusalem three times every day. Not only that, but they are praying for the restoration of God's Kingdom and for the Messiah to come. If you did know that, you might think this practice is just for the Jews and the religion of Judaism. After all, Solomon's prayer is in the Old Testament and not for anyone today … right?

You may also be surprised to find out how much time our Messiah spent in Jerusalem, traveling towards Jerusalem, and in the Temple from the time he was a little boy until his death and resurrection. Maybe you're thinking, "Yes, that's true, but it all ended when he died, right?" Well, one of the last verses in the Gospels records that as soon as Yeshua ascended to Heaven on the Mount of Olives, the disciples immediately returned to the Temple in Jerusalem, where they were daily teaching and praising God.

When the Holy Spirit fell at Pentecost, there is a good indication that the disciples were in the Temple, just as Jewish tradition would have dictated. We see later records of the disciples participating in the daily prayer service in the Temple.

Again, you might be thinking, "But Paul said that these things were done away with." Again, you may be surprised to take a

Ancient Practices for a Modern Faith

closer look and find out that Paul spent his life as a Pharisee, an observant Jew, and was careful to participate in all the traditions and practices of the Judaism of his day. We find a record of him wanting to return to Jerusalem to keep the feast of Passover after being gone on his missionary journeys for years. We also find that, just before Paul was arrested and ultimately sent to Rome, he returned to Jerusalem. While he was there, the elders told him reports were circulating that he was teaching Jewish believers that they did not need to adhere to their Jewish upbringing. To clear up any confusion, they told him to go to the Temple and participate in one of the commandments of Jewish law, offer sacrifices, and publicly prove that the rumors about his teachings were untrue.

You may be surprised to find that the practice of looking towards Jerusalem in daily prayer was something observant Jews would have done in the time of Yeshua. It should be undisputed that Yeshua and all of His disciples were observant Jews.

The point I am getting to is that you may be surprised at the Jewishness of our faith if you take a close and unbiased look at the Gospels and writings of the New Testament. We'll go into these things in more detail as we explore the second half of this book. It's important that you continue to examine what we're writing with an unbiased lens. As we begin to tie all of the things we've discussed so far together, ask God to tell you if these things are true. Don't take our word for it—search the Scriptures.

I truly believe that the ancient practices of Scripture, early Christianity, Jerusalem, and Israel should all be connected to our faith today. I believe they are important for a thriving and vibrant faith and in keeping us on the straight and narrow path that leads to God's Kingdom.

Are you ready to find out? Let's find out what Yeshua actually preached during His earthly ministry.

CHAPTER TEN

Yeshua's Message—Repent!

Zac Waller

Crack! The head of the splitting maul sank into the piece of solid oak firewood as I struck it with all the strength I could muster. It was a hard piece. Several large knots protruded from its barky side, and the grains were gnarled, twisting out from its core. Crack! Again, my maul met its mark on the knotty piece, exactly in the spot I had last struck. Finally, the obstinate log gave way, but only after cutting away a few of the tangled grains were the pieces truly separated. I tossed the split firewood into a pile and took a step back, sweaty but triumphant.

Our congregation was all out in the woods that day. We had gathered to work together and get our winter supply of wood stacked in the barn. An elder of our congregation was close by me, busy loading the pieces of split wood onto the trailer. He never missed an opportunity to use our work times together to talk about spiritual things.

"Zac," he said in his slightly high-pitched, nasally voice, "do you know what repentance means?" Without waiting for my reply, he continued, "Well, it's like this. In the British army, they marched like this, and then the commander would say "REPENT," and they would turn 180 degrees around, like this, facing the exact opposite direction. It's the same thing with sin, Zac. Once God shows you what it is, you have to turn around and walk away from it!"

I appreciated the analogy and lesson and began pondering it as I went back to splitting firewood. Sometimes repentance is pretty clear-cut. You know exactly what the sin is, and you turn away from it. But sometimes sin weaves its way into our culture, our generational line, or our theological beliefs. Though the elder's analogy certainly stands, I wondered if sometimes repentance might end up looking more like the knotty log I had been splitting than a soldier doing an about-face maneuver!

Letting go of sin can seem painful at first. When the maul drops and separates something your family has held onto for hundreds or even thousands of years, you may feel a little bit like that splintered piece of wood. Your family might think you're crazy.

You may not fit in the same places you used to. You may have to find new friends.

In our culture, there's a big emphasis on acting on what feels good now. I think this mentality has led to much immorality and is in direct opposition to repentance. The first step of repentance is to recognize sin as sin. That does not feel good. It hurts our pride and confirms our fear that we aren't able to stand alone.

So the question is, do we need to do something that hurts? I think part of our cultural problem is that we confuse "hurt" with "harm." In his book *Boundaries,* Henry Cloud shows the critical difference:

"Have you ever gone to the dentist?" I asked.
"Sure."
"Did the dentist hurt you when he drilled your tooth to remove the cavity?"
"Yes."
"Did he harm you?"
"No, he made me feel better."
"Hurt and harm are different," I pointed out. "When you ate the sugar that gave you the cavity, did that hurt?"
"No, it tasted good," he said, with a smile that told me he was catching on.
"Did it harm you?"
"Yes."

"That's my point. Things can hurt and not harm us. In fact, they can even be good for us. And things that feel good can be very harmful to us."

Is repentance a hurt that is not harmful? Let's take a look at the benefits of repentance as detailed in Scripture and find out for ourselves:

2 Corinthians 7:10: "For godly grief produces a repentance that leads to salvation."

2 Chronicles 7:14: "If my people who are called by my Name humble themselves, and pray and seek My face and turn from their wicked ways, then I will hear from heaven and will forgive their sin and heal their land."

From these Scriptures, we see that salvation—eternal life—is only obtained through repentance! When we repent and turn from our wicked ways, God hears, forgives us, and heals our land! The other thing we see is that my elder friend in the woods that day was right. Repentance isn't just verbalizing a confession, though that is critical. Repentance is also making a 180-degree turn away from sin and towards God—towards holiness, righteousness, love, etc.

This concept is also depicted in the Hebrew word for repentance: *teshuvah*. It means to return or to turn back. We have strayed

Footnote: Cloud, Henry, *Boundaries*, (Grand Rapids: HarperCollins, 2017), 96.

away from God and His intimate presence in the Garden of Eden. God has gone to great lengths to make a way of return. To do so, we must turn away from wickedness—the things that are not of God, as described in the Bible.

Unfortunately, in most of the Christian world, we have lost this element of repentance. We make a verbal confession while plunging straight ahead into sin and immorality. True repentance is to turn away from sin. With this understanding of repentance, let's take a look at a few other Scriptures:

"Yeshua began to preach, saying, 'Repent, for the kingdom of heaven is at hand'" (Matt. 4:17).

Yeshua's main message was to repent!

"She said, 'No one, Lord.' And Yeshua said, 'Neither do I condemn you; go, and from now on sin no more'" (John 8:11).

Yeshua preached that one should turn from his wicked ways:

"And Peter said to them, 'Repent and be baptized every one of you in the name of Yeshua Christ for the forgiveness of your sins, and you will receive the gift of the Holy Spirit'" (Acts 2:38).

After witnessing Yeshua's resurrection and being baptized in the Holy Spirit, Peter preached repentance!

"Repent, therefore, and turn back, that your sins may be blotted out" (Acts 3:19).

After Pentecost, Peter continued to preach *teshuvah*.

"When they heard these things they fell silent. And they glorified God, saying, 'Then to the Gentiles also God has granted repentance that leads to life'" (Acts 11:18).

The Jewish followers of Messiah were astounded to find that even the Gentiles could turn from wickedness!

The critical takeaway for us today is that turning away from sin is a necessary element of repentance, and repentance is a necessary element of salvation. In other words, you can't have salvation without turning away from evil. Just to be clear, I am not saying that we have to be perfect before God will grant us salvation. If we were perfect, we would not need salvation! What I am saying is that turning from evil is part of God's gift *in* salvation. God does not want us to remain in bondage to sin. Sin leads to death; God wants us to be free!

If we attempt to turn from evil in our own strength and do not accept God's forgiveness and salvation, we will fall into temptation and will not receive the gift of eternal life. If we do not repent but willfully continue in sin while claiming to accept God's salvation, the Scripture says:

Yeshua's Message—Repent!

"So also faith by itself, if it does not have works, is dead" (James 2:17).

In Matthew 25, Yeshua speaks about the sheep and the goats, which go to Heaven or Hell based on what they did or did not do!

An interesting point in this chapter of Matthew is that, in verse 32, He says that He will "gather the nations" and separate the sheep and the goats. So the sheep and goats could be understood as nations rather than individuals. National punishment or redemption is a biblical concept. Nineveh was judged and then spared as a nation. The nations that made war against Israel were punished as individual nations. Israel experienced exile as a punishment and is now being restored as a nation. As we mentioned before, the nations that attempted to divide the land of Israel were punished as nations.

Wickedness or repentance can produce national consequences.

Genesis 15:16 says that the Amorites' iniquity was "not yet complete." Apparently, God wanted to give the Canaanites a chance for repentance before they were punished for their iniquities as a nation.

At the end of Zechariah Chapter 14, God says that the nations that do not go to Jerusalem to worship God during the Feast of Tabernacles will be punished by not receiving any rain.

All the great awakenings, revivals, and city-wide or national transformations that the world has seen began with repentance —turning away from godlessness and towards godliness.

If we turn from wickedness, embracing God's forgiveness and eternal life, He gives us the ability to recognize sin and overcome temptation. Through the process of sanctification, we become more and more like Yeshua—the perfect, spotless Lamb of God. God's way of life, His instructions on how to live, are miraculously written on our hearts. This gives us supernatural strength to continue putting away sin and embracing righteousness.

If repentance is needed for salvation, we should know how to repent. In what areas do we need to make an about-face? Are there knotty logs in our lives that we have been putting off, that we know we need to split?

There are four main steps to repentance:

1. Recognize the sin as sin

2. Turn away from the identified sin

3. Confess the sin to God, those involved, and those you are accountable to

4. Purpose in your heart to walk in righteousness and have others hold you accountable

How do we identify what we need to repent of? In what ways has mainstream Christianity lost its biblical compass? In the following chapters, we will examine a few areas where *teshuvah* (repentance) is much needed in the Body of Messiah.

CHAPTER ELEVEN

Overcoming Rome

Zac Waller

History is a great gift. The people who lived out our history made decisions to the best of their ability, estimating but not knowing what the long-term consequences of their actions would be. We, on the other hand, can look back and analyze the full picture.

As we look back at Church history, it is important to note what changes occurred and what repercussions those changes had on the Body of Messiah and the world. By doing this, we strengthen our resolve to continue in the positive changes, correct any wrong paths we are currently on, and avoid taking wrong paths that were proven to be disastrous.

One of the main historical changes that comes to mind for most Protestant Christians is the Reformation. That was certainly a huge shift! Moving away from Catholicism and putting God's Word back into the hands of the people had an enormous effect on the world. As Protestants, we see this as a move of God and a very positive breakaway from many heresies.

But wait. Why did there need to be a reformation? The first-century Church that Yeshua and the apostles began was obviously on the right track. At what point did the Church get off track? What changes set the course for an eventual need for reformation?

I would like to focus on what I believe are the four main changes that occurred fairly early on in the life of first-century Christianity.

Relationships consist of four main elements: people, space, time, and communication. For a relationship to exist, you must have another person or people group. Secondly, there must be a place where you come together. Thirdly, there must be times when you will be together. Finally, once you are with someone, in the same place at the same time, communication launches you into interaction and begins a relationship. Remove any one of these elements, and a relationship is not possible.

Our heavenly Father created us to be in relationship with Him. Adam and Eve were the people, the cool of the day was the time, the Garden of Eden was the place, and God was intentional about communicating with His creation.

Man sinned and was removed from God's intimate presence, but God did not give up on having a relationship with His beloved humanity. It is astounding to see how fervently God has passionately pursued a relationship with us.

The first relational element we see God taking action on is choosing a people. In Genesis 12, God chose Abraham and his descendants. Through this relationship with Abraham, God wanted to bring all of humanity back into relationship with Him. Verse 3 states: "In you (Abraham) all the families of the earth shall be blessed."

God confirmed His choosing of the people of Israel as He brought them out of Egypt. Deuteronomy 7:6 says: "For you (Israel) are a people holy to the Lord your God. The Lord your God has chosen you to be a people for his treasured possession, out of all the peoples who are on the face of the earth."

Immediately after choosing Abraham, God also chose a place. In Genesis 12:1, God tells Abraham: "Go from your country and your kindred and your father's house to the land that I will show you." God took Abraham to the land of Israel.

The location gets a little more specific as the children of Israel are coming up out of Egypt. Fourteen times in the book of Deuteronomy, it speaks of "the place that the Lord your God will choose" (Deut. 12:18, 15:20, 16:7, 16:15, 17:8, 31:11). Eight times it adds "to make His Name dwell there" (Deut. 12:5, 12:11, 12:21, 14:23, 16:2, 16:6, 16:11, 26:2).

Second Chronicles 3 tells us that King Solomon built God's house in the place that God had chosen, Mount Moriah—Mount Zion.

The Psalmist writes in Chapter 132: "... the Lord has chosen Zion; he has desired it for His dwelling place: 'This is My resting place forever; here I will dwell, for I have desired it.'"

Was this place of God's choosing just a place for Him to dwell, or was the purpose to have a relationship with His people? Exodus 25:8 says: "And let them make Me a sanctuary, that I may dwell in their midst." The whole purpose of God's house was so that He could dwell in the midst of His people. He wanted a place that He could meet with His chosen people!

Though the people of Israel could come up to the Temple whenever they wanted to spend time with God, He set certain times of the year that were specially dedicated to this purpose.

"Three times in the year you shall keep a feast to me. You shall keep the Feast of Unleavened Bread. As I commanded you, you shall eat unleavened bread for seven days at the appointed time in the month of Abib, for in it you came out of Egypt. None shall appear before me empty-handed. You shall keep the Feast of Harvest, of the firstfruits of your labor, of what you sow in the field. You shall keep the Feast of Ingathering at the end of the year, when you gather in from the field the fruit of your labor. Three times in the year shall all your males appear before the Lord God" (Leviticus 23:14-17).

A people, place, and time have been designated for the people of Israel to have a relationship with Almighty God, Creator of the universe. One thing is lacking. We need some communication! It's hard enough to get to know another human being, much less the all-powerful, omnipotent God of all creation! Did God leave us in the dark? No!

God delivered the children of Israel from the bondage of Egypt and brought them to Mount Sinai where he spoke directly to them! God gave them the Ten Commandments and a whole list of loving instructions on how to have a relationship with Him and how to relate to one another. This communication enabled us to get to know Him and taught us how to relate to our fellow man.

God chose a people—Israel, a place—Israel/Jerusalem/Mount Zion, a time—the feasts, and a means of communication—His

Word so that He can "dwell among us" and we can have a relationship with Him.

Early followers of Yeshua maintained these God-given elements of relationship while fully embracing their belief in Yeshua as the long-awaited Messiah of Israel. We will discuss this more fully in the following chapter.

Roman legions destroyed God's house in 70 AD. The chosen place was gone.

Bar Kokhba was hailed by most Jews as the Messiah but was defeated by the Romans in 136 AD. This was a devastating blow to the Jewish people living in Israel and scattered them to the four corners of the earth. The chosen people were exiled.

Since the early Christians believed that Yeshua was the Messiah, they obviously did not follow Bar Kokhba or join in the revolt. This caused even more animosity between the two groups.

Brutal persecution of both Jews and Christians continued. Often, the persecution would be directed towards one faith community at a time, leaving the non-persecuted group with the choice of turning the other group in or losing their lives and their loved ones. This was another devastating blow to their relationship.

Anything that looked Jewish could cost Christians their lives. Much of God's instruction, which the Jewish people so faithfully kept, was discarded by Christians.

The Gospel continued to be preached throughout Asia and Europe. Despite the horrific persecution, many came to faith. As congregations were planted and began to grow, new leaders were needed to shepherd the flocks. Newly converted, non-Jewish Christians with limited biblical understanding and Greco-Roman mindsets filled the positions.

The Hebrew Bible was written to Hebrews. The Israelite culture was based around actions: you are what you do. In stark contrast, the Greco-Roman mindset focused more on the mind, philosophy, and ideas: you are what you believe. This pushed Christian theologies further away from God's Word—His loving instructions on how to live and have relationships.

In 306 AD, Constantine became Emperor of the Roman Empire. By 323 AD, Christianity had become Rome's official religion.

The effect all these things had on Christianity was immense. In just 300 years, God's chosen people were scattered around the world, sure to assimilate, just like every other nation in history that had experienced exile. God's chosen place was forgotten, and now Rome, the very city that had destroyed her, claimed to have taken her place. God's holy feasts had all but ceased or been replaced by pagan festivals. God's Word, His holy instructions, had been thrown to the wayside and declared obsolete.

"Replacement theology" has been embraced by most of Christianity from the third century until this day. It has been defined as replacing the Jewish people with the Church as God's chosen people. I would take it a step further and say that the ramifications of embracing replacement theology have led us to also reject and replace all four of the elements of relationship with God. It is unthinkable that man would decide he had a right to reject and replace the beautiful elements of relationship God Himself had established.

The Protestant Reformation was critical to addressing this tragedy. It put God's Word back into the hands of the people. I believe that was one of God's first steps in restoring His relationship with us.

The Word has been restored, but what about the other elements—the people, the place, and the times? What would it be like to put these relationally-critical elements back where God designed them to be? Did God's fundamental basis for relationship change when the Messiah came?

CHAPTER TWELVE

Returning to Our Roots

Zac Waller

Towering, majestic timbers have always held a special place in my heart. When I was a boy, we had three giant oaks in our front yard. They were massive and provided a wonderful canopy of shade. An observer would have concluded that we would never tire of playing on a swing my father had fastened to its burly limbs. I remember lying on the ground and staring up into the branches, in awe of God's beautiful, artistic, and powerful handiwork.

I often wondered what the root structure of these gigantic trees must look like. In order to support its limbs, a tree of its size must have about as much under the ground as it had on top, I reasoned. Though I was curious, there was no easy way to find out what lay beneath the surface. I so wished that I could have a map or diagram of exactly what the roots looked like and how they had formed over the years. Of course, no such thing existed for that particular tree.

A growing movement of Christians is desiring this very thing in relation to our faith. What is beneath the surface of the towering tree of Christianity? Without the solid foundation of a healthy root structure, surely this tree will not survive for long. Could this be why we have seen such a falling away among our young people? Have we committed faith suicide by detaching ourselves from the nourishing stability of our own roots?

Like the tree in my front yard growing up, the roots of our faith have been hidden beneath the surface, unclear to the casual observer and willfully ignored by arrogant branches.

Unlike the tree in my story, we do have a map revealing, in great detail, what this root structure is, why it is, and how it has developed over the years. Though greatly ignored by many branches of Christianity, the Bible very clearly declares God's purposes for the entirety of His planting—roots, branches, and all.

I say "greatly ignored" because the Bible has not been completely ignored by most Christians. The majority of Christians will look to the New Testament and declare that their roots began there, with the birth of the Messiah. A closer look at the New Testament writings reveals that the roots of Christianity go much deeper!

Let's start with the very first verse, Matthew 1:1:
"The book of the genealogy of Yeshua Christ, the son of David, the son of Abraham."

Right from the start, the New Testament reveals that its roots are David and Abraham! But we cannot base a whole doctrine on one verse. Let's see if there are other verses that confirm this concept.

In the very first chapter of Luke, Mary praises God and declares in verses 54-55:
"He has helped his servant Israel, in remembrance of his mercy, as he spoke to our fathers, to Abraham and to his offspring forever."

Mary knew that the Messiah whom she would bring into the world was connected to Abraham.

Galatians 3:7-9 says:

"Know then that it is those of faith who are the sons of Abraham. And the Scripture, foreseeing that God would justify the Gentiles by faith, preached the gospel beforehand to Abraham, saying,

"In you shall all the nations be blessed." So then, those who are of faith are blessed along with Abraham, the man of faith." Abraham heard the Gospel?

For centuries, Christians have seen everything that happened before Messiah came as leading up to Him. Once He came, He changed everything and began a totally new movement. I believe this is biblically inaccurate. Yeshua was part of the plan from the very beginning. His plans were Abraham's plans, and His work was a continuation of what He had called and enabled Abraham to do. This is a very big shift. The biblical x-rays beneath the surface of the tree of Christianity have revealed that our roots extend all the way to Abraham.

If the Abrahamic tree was chopped, burned, and replaced when Yeshua came, then Abraham becomes irrelevant. If Yeshua is the continuation of the root of Abraham, then we could learn a great deal about who Yeshua is by what He did through Abraham. If we disconnect from our roots, we commit faith suicide.

After the death and resurrection of Yeshua, the apostles James and Paul both referred to Abraham as "our father" (James 2:21 & Romans 4:16). In the parable of the rich man and Lazarus, Yeshua Himself used the term "Abraham's bosom" as a synonym for Heaven! We also see Yeshua using "our father" in reference to Abraham. At the end of this parable, Yeshua teaches something very interesting. The rich man calls out to Abraham, saying, "'I beg you, father, to send him (Lazarus) to my father's house. I have five brothers—so that he may warn them, lest they also come into this place of torment.' But Abraham said, 'They have Moses and the Prophets; let them hear them.' And he said, 'No, father Abraham, but if someone goes to them from the dead, they will repent.' He said to him, 'If they do not hear Moses and the Prophets, neither will they be convinced if someone should rise from the dead'" (Luke 16:27-31).

Yeshua is clearly saying in this parable that, if you want to get to Heaven, you need to repent and listen to Moses and the Prophets!

Abraham's, Moses', all the Prophets' and Yeshua's mission was to reconcile man's relationship with God. As Yeshua put it, "May Your kingdom come and Your will be done on Earth as it is in Heaven" (Matt. 6:10).

Abraham did this by having faith in God, dedicating his descendants for God's purposes, going to Canaan, and starting a movement that would impact the world. Moses fulfilled his mission by bringing the people of Israel into the land of Israel and giving them the Word of God. Yeshua provided atonement for our sins and gave us eternal life.

These are all the same mission! They are all God's work on the earth! They are not contradictory. They are the roots that keep us planted, the firm foundation that our faith is built upon. The burning question now is what bearing this connectivity had on the early Church and what effect it should have on Christians today.

CHAPTER THIRTEEN

Christians in the Synagogues

Zac Waller

"You have arrived at your destination," declared the GPS. Our hosts welcomed us and beautifully demonstrated the warm hospitality that the southern United States is known for.

"Projector, information table, got my speaking notes printed off. Alright, I think we're all set!"

It was a full house. People had come from all around to hear about our work in Israel. Things were going wonderfully. My two friends and I laid it all out, declaring the faithfulness of God to His people Israel the miraculous restoration of the land of Israel that is happening in our day, and why Christians should join the movement.

After our presentation, we opened up the floor for Q&A. An elderly lady raised her hand and said with a beautiful, deeply emotional southern drawl, "I have enjoyed seeing the passion you young men have for God, but it's all about Yeshua. You just can't add anything to Yeshua!" Tears welled up in her eyes and she repeated, "It's all about Yeshua!"

At that moment, I realized two things. First, most Christians have dedicated their lives to someone they know very little about and, secondly, they see Yeshua as the one who gave them eternal life but largely ignore His will for His people on this earth.

To overcome this ignorance, we have to get back to the Word! Who was Yeshua? What did He stand for? What was His will for His people and this earth?

Biblically, we know for sure that Yeshua is the Messiah, the Son of God. He is fully human and divine. He was from the beginning. He will be until the end! Yeshua's will and the Father's will are one.

Therefore, it was Yeshua's plan of salvation to (1) choose Abraham, his descendants, and the land of Israel, (2) give His people the Torah, (3) send them the words of the prophets, (4) die for the remission of our sins, (5) give us eternal life, (6) partially harden the Jewish people until the message of the Gospel reaches the fullness of the nations, (7) restore His land and people—Israel, (8) reveal Himself as the Messiah to His Jewish brothers, and (9) bring all the nations of the world to worship the God of Israel in Jerusalem!

That's the 10,000-foot view of who He is. But who was He on this earth? What did He do? What was His culture? He is to be our example in everything. Who is He?

"The book of the genealogy of Yeshua Messiah (Yeshua Christ), the Son of David, the Son of Abraham:" (Matt.1:1).

Yeshua is Jewish! He is the "Lion of the tribe of Judah." It is no coincidence that Yeshua was born into a Jewish family. He practiced Jewish culture and tradition. That was his way of life. "Joseph also went up from Galilee, out of the city of Nazareth, into Judea, to the city of David, which is called Bethlehem ... with Mary, his betrothed wife, who was with child ... So it was ... she brought forth her firstborn Son, and wrapped Him in swaddling clothes, and laid Him in a manger" (Luke 2:4-7). Yeshua was born in the city of Bethlehem, in the province of Judea, in the land of Israel, exactly as the prophets foretold. The location is extremely significant. Abraham was told to go to Canaan. Jacob (who would be later renamed Israel) left Laban in Haran and went to Canaan. The children of Israel went out of Egypt and back to the land of Israel. It should not be overlooked that Yeshua, the Messiah, the Son of God, was born in Israel! In fact, other than His journey down into Egypt as a child, our Savior spent his entire life, including all of His ministry years, in the land of Israel. The literal, physical, geographical location of Israel is critical in God's master plan of salvation for the world. "And when eight days were completed for the circumcision of the Child, His name was called Yeshua, the name given by the angel before He was conceived in the womb" (Luke 2:21).

Yeshua was circumcised. God's perfect and loving instruction in the Torah is for male children to be circumcised on the eighth day. Yeshua did not go against His Father's instruction.

"Now when the days of her purification according to the law of Moses were completed, they brought Him to Jerusalem to present Him to the Lord (as it is written in the law of the Lord, 'Every male who opens the womb shall be called holy to the Lord'), and to offer a sacrifice according to what is said in the law of the Lord, 'A pair of turtledoves or two young pigeons'" (Luke 2:22-24).

Yeshua was redeemed. Again, Yeshua perfectly fulfilled His Father's word, even as an infant.

"Now so it was that after three days they found Him in the temple, sitting in the midst of the teachers, both listening to them and asking them questions. And all who heard Him were astonished at His understanding and answers. So when they saw Him, they were amazed; and His mother said to Him, 'Son, why have You done this to us? Look, Your father and I have sought You anxiously.' And He said to them, 'Why did you seek Me? Did you not know that I must be about My Father's business?' But they did not understand the statement which He spoke to them" (Luke 2:46-50).

Yeshua studied in the Temple. God-fearing Jews would gather in the Temple courts for prayer and the study of God's Word. Yeshua went to His Father's house to be part of this with his Jewish family and to be about His Father's business.

"So He came to Nazareth, where He had been brought up. And as His custom was, He went into the synagogue on the Sabbath day, and stood up to read"(Luke 4:16).

Yeshua worshipped in the synagogue with the Pharisees every Saturday! Many will be quick to point out the times Yeshua rebukes the Pharisees or they do something wrong. The reality is that they were Yeshua's family. They were his people. He was with them on a regular basis. If Yeshua came to your town today, His custom would be to find the local synagogue and go there on Saturdays to pray and study with His brothers!

"Then He took the five loaves and the two fish, and looking up to heaven, He blessed and broke them, and gave them to the disciples to set before the multitude" (Luke 9:16).

The Torah commands us to bless God for the land after we have eaten and are satisfied (Deut. 8:10). Yeshua kept the Jewish tradition of blessing God for food before he ate!

"Our Father in heaven, Hallowed be Your name. Your kingdom come. Your will be done on earth as it is in heaven. Give us this day our daily bread. And forgive us our debts, as we forgive our debtors. And do not lead us into temptation, but deliver us from the evil one. For Yours is the kingdom and the power and the glory forever. Amen" (Matthew 6:8-13).

Yeshua taught His disciples to pray traditional Jewish prayers. The content and format of the "Our Father" prayer is very similar to other liturgical Pharisaic prayers of Yeshua's day.

"And when he had said these things, as they were looking on, he was lifted up, and a cloud took him out of their sight. And while they were gazing into heaven as he went, behold, two men stood by them in white robes, and said, 'Men of Galilee, why do you stand looking into heaven? This Yeshua, who was taken up from you into heaven, will come in the same way as you saw him go into heaven'" (Acts 1:9-11).

Yeshua is coming back to Israel! Even when Yeshua returns to this earth, Israel will be the focal point.

What about after Yeshua died and was resurrected? Did the apostles live as Jews?

"For Moses has had throughout many generations those who preach him in every city, being read in the synagogues every Sabbath" (Acts 15:21).

In the debate over whether Gentiles should keep God's instructions given to the Jews—the Torah—James states that Gentiles should start with four main things and then continue learning every Shabbat in the synagogue. Not only were the Jews supposed to continue worshipping in the synagogues, the non-Jews were to do so, as well:

"... They (James and the elders in Jerusalem) said to him (Paul), "You see, brother, how many myriads of Jews there are who have believed, and they are all zealous for the law; but they have been informed about you that you teach all the Jews who are among the Gentiles to forsake Moses, saying that they ought not to circumcise their children nor to walk according to the customs. What then? The assembly must certainly meet, for they will hear that you have come. Therefore do what we tell you: We have four men who have taken a vow. Take them and be purified with them, and pay their expenses so that they may shave their heads, and that all may know that those things of which they were informed concerning you are nothing, but that you yourself also walk orderly and keep the law" (Acts 21:20-24).

Jews who had accepted Yeshua as their Messiah were zealous for the laws of God—and that was a good thing! James and the elders in Jerusalem asked Paul to prove that he had not taught the Jews who were among the Gentiles to abandon the commandments. This would encourage the Jews to continue in their zeal for God's Word and His ways.

"So continuing daily with one accord in the temple, and breaking bread from house to house, they ate their food with gladness and simplicity of heart" (Acts 2:46).

After Yeshua's death and resurrection and after the Holy Spirit had come, the followers of Yeshua continued to gather daily in the Temple!

"... But took leave of them, saying, 'I must by all means keep this coming feast in Jerusalem; but I will return again to you, God willing.' And he sailed from Ephesus" (Acts 18:21).

Paul was not going to miss his appointments with God! There are more examples, but through those quoted here, we can see that Yeshua and the early Church did not forsake the people, place, times and Word that God had previously established. They did not reject or replace any of them but embraced them as elements of relationship with God.

If we want to "arrive at our destination," I believe it is time for the Body of Messiah to do some "recalculating." We need to acknowledge our roots, realign ourselves with God's perfect ways, and actively bring His kingdom to Earth!

To those who say that I'm adding to Yeshua by acknowledging these elements, I have a question for you. Which of these elements will not be a part of Yeshua's kingdom when He comes to reign from Jerusalem? If they all will be, then we should learn about them and come to understand the ways of our Master! Speaking of God's kingdom on Earth, I think the hardest element of relationship to understand, for all of us who have lost our direction, is the place. Why would God choose a specific geographical location?

CHAPTER FOURTEEN

Loving God's Chosen Place

Zac Waller

Sitting on the floor of my grandparent's cabin, not far from Hopkinsville, Kentucky, I turned the dial of an old-fashioned radio receiver. I was thirteen years old and had come to help Papa with some remodeling on his house.

"Welcome to Adventures in Odyssey!" crackled through the old speakers. Having grown up in a devout Christian family, I was somewhat familiar with this Christian radio program and was excited to listen and find out what adventure would be taking place tonight at Whit's End.

I had been baptized in our church at the age of four after a presentation called "Heaven's Gates and Hell's Flames." I was sure that I didn't want to go to Hell! Now, at thirteen, as I listened to the story of how Eugene Meltsner from *Adventures in Odyssey* gave his life to Yeshua, I thought, "You know, I got baptized mainly out of fear, but I'm not so sure I fully committed myself to serve God."

God really moved my heart to long for His ways. I wanted to be part of building His kingdom on this earth. The Holy Spirit was convicting me of being okay with being okay. I felt God calling me higher. He wanted me to live a life that would show His light in my life and enable me to be productive in His kingdom.

A couple weeks later, I was baptized for the second time, committing myself to God's service and the overcoming power of the blood of the Lamb.

I dove headlong into the Scriptures and felt an urge to get more serious about worship. I had been plunking around on a guitar for a year or so and was just getting to where I could play a song or two.

One day, I decided to take a psalm and put it to music. Our family had been studying and learning about Israel for several years, and something drew me to Psalm 137. I had never written a song before, but something was bubbling up within me, and I needed to let it out!

In very few minutes, the tune came to me, and I scribbled these words on a piece of paper:

"Jerusalem, Jerusalem, pray for the peace of Jerusalem.

If I forget you, Jerusalem, let my right hand forget her cunning.

If I do not remember you, let my tongue cling to the roof of my mouth,

If I prefer not Jerusalem above my chief joy."

Though I had never been to Jerusalem, something about this passage really pulled at my freshly-born heartstrings. There was something about this city that I could not explain, but my heart knew. There was some sort of yearning burning within my newly-committed and innocent soul. Little did I know then where this yearning would lead.

Seven years later, I found myself standing in Jerusalem at the Western Wall. As I prayed and backed away from the wall, it was a surreal moment. On one hand, I could feel that there was something going on here that was beyond my comprehension, while on the other hand, it was just a really cool, historic rock wall.

Over the following years, Scriptures about this place would jump out at me.

Psalms 32:13-14:

"For the Lord has chosen Zion; He has desired it for His dwelling place: 'This is My resting place forever; Here I will dwell, for I have desired it.'"

Zechariah 8:1-3:

"Again the word of the Lord of hosts came, saying,'Thus says the Lord of hosts: I am zealous for Zion with great zeal; With great fervor I am zealous for her.' 'Thus says the Lord: 'I will return to Zion, And dwell in the midst of Jerusalem. Jerusalem shall be called the City of Truth, The Mountain of the Lord of hosts, The Holy Mountain.'"

Mark 11:15-17:

"So they came to Jerusalem. Then Yeshua went into the temple and began to drive out those who bought and sold in the temple, and overturned the tables of the money changers and the seats of those who sold doves. And He would not allow anyone to carry wares through the temple. Then He taught, saying to them, 'Is it not written, 'My house shall be called a house of prayer for all nations'?"

John 2:14-17:

"And He found in the temple those who sold oxen and sheep and doves, and the money changers doing business. When He had made a whip of cords, He drove them all out of the temple, with the sheep and the oxen, and poured out the changers' money and overturned the tables. And He said to those who sold doves, 'Take these things away! Do not make My Father's house a house of merchandise!' Then His disciples remembered that it was written, 'Zeal for Your house has eaten Me up.'"

Luke 2:42-48:

"And when He was twelve years old, they went up to Jerusalem according to the custom of the feast. When they had finished the days, as they returned, the Boy Yeshua lingered behind in Jerusalem. And Joseph and His mother did not know it; but supposing Him to have been in the company, they went a day's journey, and sought Him among their relatives and acquaintances. So when they did not find Him, they returned to Jerusalem, seeking Him. Now so it was that after three days they found Him in the temple, sitting in the midst of the teachers, both listening to them and asking them questions. And all who heard Him were astonished at His understanding and answers. So when they saw Him, they were amazed; and His mother said to Him, 'Son, why have You done this to us? Look, Your father and I have sought You anxiously.' And He said to them, 'Why did you seek Me? Did you not know that I must be about My Father's business?'"

Acts 2:46-47:

"So continuing daily with one accord in the Temple, and breaking bread from house to house, they ate their food with gladness and simplicity of heart, praising God and having favor with all the people."

God chose Jerusalem. The prophets were passionate about it. Yeshua didn't want to leave it and was zealous for it. The disciples were in the Temple every day! There is certainly something supernaturally significant about this specific geographical location.

But why? Why is it necessary for God to choose a specific place? God met me in rural Kentucky. Is it really necessary for me to connect to Jerusalem? It seems like my relationship with God could be fine without it. Though God's judgments are unsearchable and His ways past finding out (Romans 11:33), I believe there are some things we can see in the Scriptures that will give us good, solid answers.

God created man and placed him in the Garden of Eden. From the very beginning, there was a place. In this place, God was able to be with man.

"And they heard the sound of the Lord God walking in the garden in the cool of the day" (Genesis 3:8).

We know the story well. Man sinned, and two cherubim were stationed at the gate of the garden, blocking man from re-entering the intimate presence of the Lord. It is important to note here that God still communicated with mankind outside of the garden (Genesis 4:6)! God could reach outside the garden to man, but man could not go back into the garden with God. What was the chain holding man from re-entering the garden? Sin. God cannot tolerate sin.

God continued to speak to anyone who would listen. Finally, Abraham showed up on the scene. He chose not only to listen but to walk before God. Now God had a man willing to obey him (the opposite of sin). Could God use a willing man to bring about the reconciliation of all mankind? Yes. Abraham started that movement, and that's why we call him Father Abraham.

What was Abraham's first assignment on this road to recovery from sin? "Go to a land that I will show you" (Gen. 12:1). God took Abraham to Israel.

Moses led the children of Israel up out of the land of Egypt. On the way, God said, "Make Me a sanctuary, that I may dwell among them" (Ex. 25:8).

Through the service of the Tabernacle, the high priest, who represented all the children of Israel, was able to enter into the Holy of Holies, approach the two cherubim stationed on the ark, and enter into God's intimate presence.

God wants more than just the ability to speak to us from Heaven. He wants to be with us! That is what He created us for! God can spiritually be with us anywhere in the world. He can speak to us anywhere in the world. God chose Jerusalem so that we have a place to be together physically, so that we can come into the intimate presence of God!

As Christians, we might reason, "I no longer need a physical location because Yeshua has brought me into the intimate presence of God right where I'm at." I want to make one thing very clear. Meeting God in Jerusalem does not take away from the great work that Yeshua did by shedding His blood for us!

Yeshua's sacrifice is perfectly in line with everything I've written. It is the continuation of God's plan of reconciling man back to God.

Yeshua's death paid the price for our sins and gives eternal life to all those who accept Him. Through His death, He has also given us the power to overcome sin in this world. Eternal life and sanctification are incredible gifts from God! Eternal life allows us to be in God's presence for all of eternity. Sanctification is a process that takes place here on Earth. None of us are without sin. It takes a daily walk of sanctification to become more and more like Yeshua.

Because of the reality of sin in this world, we cannot experience the intimate presence of God without a chosen place with a set protocol of holiness. We still need the Temple for God to come and dwell with us in that way.

Yes, Yeshua is with us and we have the Holy Spirit. But if the full presence of God manifested itself right now in our midst, we would all fall down dead! God is perfect in all of His ways. He loves us so much that He chose a place so that even in our sin, we can come close to Him.

Luke 9:53 speaks of the Samaritans who did not receive Yeshua "because His face was set for the journey to Jerusalem."

Acts 18 describes how Paul sailed from Ephesus saying, "I must by all means keep this coming feast in Jerusalem."

Based on Isaiah 56 and Yeshua's words in Mark 11, the end goal is for all nations to come up to Jerusalem to pray and be joyful in God's house!

At the end of the day, God has chosen Jerusalem! Even if we don't understand everything, God has big plans for this chosen city, and we would do well to align ourselves with Him and His plans!

I hope this chapter has challenged you to dig more into this topic. There are many great resources that dig even further, including the book *Yeshua Loves the Temple* by Ben Hilton.

Whatever path God takes you on from here, my prayer for you is that you find yourself drawing ever closer to our heavenly Father through Yeshua our Messiah.

CHAPTER FIFTEEN

Loving God's Word

Zac Waller

Frustrated, I laid the concordance down on my desk. I couldn't find it anywhere! For about an hour, I had searched the Scriptures and used every concordance and lexicon I had available. Still, nothing made sense. I believe it was *Nave's Topical Bible* that had come the closest. Under "Sabbath," there were pages of references. At the very end of the "Sabbath" section was the title "Christian Sabbath" and, beneath it, three verses:

"I was in the Spirit on the Lord's Day, and I heard behind me a loud voice, as of a trumpet" (Revelation 1:10).

"Now on the first day of the week, when the disciples came together to break bread, Paul, ready to depart the next day, spoke to them and continued his message until midnight" (Acts 20:7).

"On the first day of the week let each one of you lay something aside, storing up as he may prosper, that there be no collections when I come" (1 Corinthians 16:2).

Either some theologians were way off the mark, or my thirteen-year-old brain was not sophisticated enough to understand the depths of Scripture. I took a deep breath, stood up from my desk, walked downstairs, and asked, "Dad, where do people get that the Sabbath was changed from Saturday to Sunday? I can't find anything in the Bible that says anything like that!"

Dad explained how the Roman Emperor Constantine had changed it in order to get away from anything Jewish and to help the pagan sun worshippers unite under his new style of Christianity. Later church fathers had to come up with some biblical reason for the switch, so they took these three verses as their "proof."

"It is very easy to prove from the Scriptures that God Himself set the seventh day apart and that all the holy men of the Bible, from Moses to the apostles, kept that day as the Sabbath. And that's why we started keeping Saturday as the Sabbath five years ago," he finished.

I couldn't, for the life of me, figure out why anyone would be resistant to the Sabbath! Shabbat had become a very special day in our home. On Friday nights, Mom would prepare a special candlelit dinner. Dad would pray a blessing over each of us. Saturdays were spent in fellowship with God, studying, worshiping, and in prayer with fellow believers.

It was a day of physical rest, but more importantly, it was a glimpse into the future day when death will be no more—no more sorrow and no more pain. It was a day to cease from our labors and consider what we had been laboring for. It was a day to remember what we had in the Garden of Eden and to launch us into the next six days of labor wherein we strive to return the world to that state.

All the feasts of the Lord were designed to bring us together with God. Why would we not show up for these God-ordained appointments? I believe it is because we have disregarded one of the other elements of relationship—God's Word. It grieves my heart to think of all the hurt and pain we have endured as the Body of Messiah by believing the heresy that God's breathed word was "done away with." The Torah is a special treasure given to man in order to know God. The Torah shows us who He is and what He says is right and wrong. It is not just a list of rules to follow; it is a guidebook for success and fulfillment! There are many debates over whether Jews are obligated to keep all the commandments of God. Nowadays, we are discussing the responsibilities of us non-Jews. Are we obligated, forbidden, invited ...?

The purpose of this chapter is not to dive into those topics but to simply state that the instruction found in the Torah is God's breathed Word and should be respected as such!

Second Timothy 3:16-17 says, "All Scripture is given by inspiration of God, and is profitable for doctrine, for reproof, for correction, for instruction in righteousness, that the man of God may be complete, thoroughly equipped for every good work." The New Testament was not written yet! Paul is speaking of the Tanakh—the Torah, the Writings, and the Prophets.

I can personally testify that I have been abundantly blessed by walking in the "instruction in righteousness" that the Torah offers! Choosing a moral compass based on God's Word is a stabilizing, life-changing, and eternity-affecting decision! So many relationships are crashing and burning. People are being abused in the worst ways. Families are falling apart. Can we embrace Yeshua's gift of writing God's law on our hearts? Our fear of being legalistic, our inability to take correction, and our aversion to humbly receiving loving instructions is drowning us

Loving God's Word

and our children in immorality! God's Word still stands. Through Yeshua the Messiah, He's extending a life rope to all those willing to lay down their pride and allow the Holy Spirit to write God's loving instructions on their hearts.

I have a lot of respect for my dad, Tommy Waller. He had the guts to acknowledge that he needed the life rope. Dad is the greatest example I know of in keeping his heart open for God to make impressions and, through them, to write His law on Dad's heart.

Through other people, God's Word, and the Holy Spirit speaking into his life, Dad would see areas that he needed to change, and he would change! They say that the definition of insanity is doing the same thing over and over again, expecting different results. Dad has chosen not to live a life of insanity!

He recognized that sexual immorality was an issue in the Church, so he decided to search the Scriptures to see what we could do differently. We embraced the ancient method of marriage called "betrothal" (not to be confused with "arranged marriage"). These testimonies are written down in the books *Betrothed* and *Beloved*.

Dad recognized that disengaged fatherhood is an issue in the Church, so he quit his management position with FedEx and became a farmer. Through this, he was able to interact with, teach, and love us—his children. This blessing, approval, and mentorship from Dad proved to have an incredibly positive impact on our lives.

Dad recognized that anti-Semitism is still alive and well in the Church, so he moved our whole family to Israel, and we began blessing, loving, and supporting the Orthodox Jews. Through this, we began to learn much more about Jewish/Christian history and have been able to be a voice of education to the Christian world.

There are more steps he took, but my point is that each of these major decisions was made because Dad compared current situations to the Word of God. When they did not line up, he made changes! Without the plumb line of the Word, there's no way to know what to change!

By accepting God's Word as the compass that we calibrate our lives to, we come into closer relationship with Him, and those we love will be positively affected.

If you are believing theologies that have not been proven with the Word of God, I challenge you: please go, as I did at thirteen, and search the Scriptures. Then find someone you can talk to about it. God's Word is the standard! As you study, His word will become a lamp unto your feet and a light to your path (Psalm 119:105).

CHAPTER SIXTEEN

Loving God's Chosen People

Zac Waller

"Har Bracha?" I yelled through the open door and over the rumble of the engine. "*Ken* (Yes), Bracha!" the bus driver hollered back. Four of my brothers and I boarded the bus headed from Ariel to the Mount of Blessing (Har Bracha), deep in the heart of Samaria.

Brayden, the oldest of us brothers, was the most passionate about learning the Hebrew language. As soon as he was on the bus, he began scanning the passengers to see if there were any Israeli candidates for Hebrew practice.

An elder gentleman with a long white beard and friendly eyes sat not too many seats away. "*Ma shlomcha?* (How are you?)"

Brayden asked. "*Baruch HaShem*! (Praise God!)" the man replied.

After a few minutes of very small talk, the conversation switched to English. "So, who are you guys?" he asked.

"We are Bible-believing Christians, and we've come to help the farmers here in Israel's Heartland."

"Wait. So, you've come to support the Jews living here in Samaria?"

"Yes, we believe that God's covenant with Abraham and his descendants still stands today!"

"Wow, this is very interesting. The only things I know about Christians are from the stories I heard from my grandfather who lived in Lithuania. My grandfather said that Christians would come out on their Jewish holidays and break down their doors and windows, drag them out on the streets, and beat them mercilessly. I have always believed that Christians hate us Jews."

At that point, I wasn't very knowledgeable about the tragic history of Jewish persecution by those who called themselves Christians. This encounter struck a chord deep in my heart. Yeshua, the one I know as Messiah and Savior, was viewed among the Jewish people as someone who wanted to see them all horrifically tortured and annihilated. My heart ached at this terrible misrepresentation of Yeshua. He was a righteous Jew who walked in love, even towards his enemies. How could this have happened?

In order to understand this Jew-hatred, commonly know as anti-Semitism, we need to go all the way back to the book of Exodus. In chapter 17, we read about how the Amalekites attacked the people of Israel. At the end of the chapter, it says: "... the LORD has sworn: the LORD will have war with Amalek from generation to generation."

In the book of Deuteronomy, we get a little more information on why Amalek was singled out. In Deuteronomy 25:17-18, God says, "Remember what Amalek did to you on the way as you were coming out of Egypt, how he met you on the way and attacked your rear ranks, all the stragglers at your rear, when you were tired and weary; and he did not fear God."

What does it mean that God Himself would war against Amalek from generation to generation? Let's take a look at history and see if we can find some clues.

Sure enough, the Amalekites appear again and again as the enemies of Israel. Joshua, King Saul, and King David all fought battles against them. In the book of Esther, we find that Haman was an "Agagite." Agag was the king of the Amalekites in King Saul's day.

Once again, against all odds, God miraculously delivered the Jewish people from destruction. Though we don't know the exact lineage of Amalek, this generation to generation obsession with fighting against God by attempting to annihilate His people has been carried on by the Greeks, Romans, Byzantines, Arabs, Crusaders, Mamluks, Nazis, and—today—by most of Israel's neighboring Arab countries, as well as the Arabs living within Israel (the so-called "Palestinians").

Many of the Romans, all of the Byzantines and Crusaders, and many of the Nazis who committed unspeakable atrocities towards the Jewish people proclaimed to be Christian followers of Yeshua.

As Christians, we could try to dismiss any responsibility on our part by saying that these people could not have been real Christians! This may be true, but it does not take away the fact that their actions were done in Yeshua's name. Some Christians might say that these perpetrators were just Christian in name only and could not have been serious about their faith. Let's take a look at the words of John Chrysostom, a prominent church father of the fourth century:

"But these Jews are gathering choruses of effeminates and a great rubbish heap of harlots. ...The synagogue is not only a brothel and a theater; it also is a den of robbers and a lodging for wild beasts. ... Demons dwell in the synagogue, not only in

Footnote: Chrysostom, John, *Against the Jews, Homily 1*, 2:7, 6:6, 7:5, turtullian.org, 2011, http://www.tertullian.org/fathers/chrysostom_adversus_judaeos_01_homily1.htm

the place itself but also in the souls of the Jews. ... For I am persuaded to call the fasting of the Jews a table of demons because they slew God."

As Protestant Christians, we could say that these were Catholic heresies that were overcome by the Reformation.

Let's see what Martin Luther himself had to say about the Jews:

"First, their synagogues should be set on fire. ... Secondly, their homes should likewise be broken down and destroyed. ... Thirdly, they should be deprived of their prayer books and Talmuds in which such idolatry, lies, cursing, and blasphemy are taught. ... Fifthly, traveling privileges must be absolutely forbidden to Jews. ... If however we are afraid that they might harm us personally ... then let us settle with them for that which they have extorted usuriously from us, and after having divided it up fairly, let us drive them out of the country for all time."

We can clearly see that our forefathers made some serious mistakes, and those mistakes were very costly. The question for us is, what do we do now? What is the right Christian view of the Jewish people? They do not accept Yeshua as the Messiah. Can we support them in that state?

In an effort to answer those questions, some have embraced

Footnote: Franklin Sherman, ed., *Luther's Works, Volume 47: The Christian in Society IV* (Philadelphia: Fortress Press, 1971), 268-293.

"dual covenant" theology. This doctrine states that the Jews have a covenant outside the new covenant in Yeshua the Messiah that permits them a place in the world to come.

There are many biblical holes in this theology, and even the writers of it have recanted much of what they first proposed. In my opinion, dual covenant theology does not qualify as biblically sound.

Today, with the miraculous restoration of Israel and the regathering of the Jewish people to their ancient homeland, another big question has arisen. If the Jewish people are lost and without God because of their denial of Yeshua as Messiah, why is God blessing them, fulfilling His promise that if they turned to Him, He would restore them?

Many of us Christians, after getting to know the God-fearing, Orthodox Jewish Zionist community, have also had to face some hard questions. Christianity has always painted a picture of Jews that don't accept Yeshua as their Messiah as arrogant, legalistic, judgmental Pharisees who hate everything Yeshua stood for. This is not what we have found!

Orthodox Jewish Zionists love God! They pray fervent prayers to their heavenly Father, study God's Holy Word with great passion, and live their lives in service to their Creator. They are passionate about loving God and their fellow man. They have sacrificed everything to fulfill the will of their Beloved—to settle the land of Israel and be a light to the nations.

At this point, I think it's a good time to broach the question "Why do they reject Yeshua as the Messiah?" There are plenty of materials out there from the Orthodox community explaining why they don't believe, so I will not add to that. Instead, I will stick to what I think our perspective as Christians should be.

Romans 11 is the go-to chapter for understanding this "mystery," as Paul describes it.

In verse 25, Paul says: "For I do not desire, brethren, that you should be ignorant of this mystery, lest you should be wise in your own opinion, that blindness in part has happened to Israel until the fullness of the Gentiles has come in."

In this verse, we see that God Himself put partial blindness on the Jewish people so that the message of salvation would be launched out into the nations. In other words, the reason why I, a man from Tennessee, have heard the Gospel is that the Jewish people rejected Yeshua as the Messiah. This begs the question, "Did God send all the Jews from Yeshua's first coming until the 'fullness of the Gentile' to Hell so that all of us from the nations could hear the Gospel?"

Verses 26 and 27 continue: "And so all Israel will be saved, as it is written: 'The Deliverer will come out of Zion, And He will turn away ungodliness from Jacob; For this is My covenant with them, When I take away their sins.'"

"The Deliverer will come from Zion" —This sounds like the second coming of Yeshua! We see a description of this in Zechariah 12:8-11:

"In that day the Lord will defend the inhabitants of Jerusalem; the one who is feeble among them in that day shall be like David, and the house of David shall be like God, like the Angel of the Lord before them. It shall be in that day that I will seek to destroy all the nations that come against Jerusalem.

And I will pour on the house of David and on the inhabitants of Jerusalem the Spirit of grace and supplication; then they will look on Me whom they pierced. Yes, they will mourn for Him as one mourns for his only son, and grieve for Him as one grieves for a firstborn. In that day there shall be a great mourning in Jerusalem, like the mourning at Hadad Rimmon in the plain of Megiddo."

It's important to notice here that God is defending the Jews in Jerusalem before they "Look on [Him] whom they pierced."

Back to Romans 11, let's continue with verse 28:

"Concerning the gospel they are enemies for your sake, but concerning the election they are beloved for the sake of the fathers."

Again, we are reminded that their rejection is for our benefit. The next part is quite interesting. What do "election" and "beloved" mean? Perhaps "election" is just saying that they are God's chosen people, or maybe it means that God has a special grace for those whom He partially hardened for our sake. Perhaps these God-fearing Jews who are doing everything that God has revealed to them would fall into a similar category as those who were born before Yeshua came into the world?

Yeshua said of Abraham: "Abraham rejoiced that he would see my day. He saw it and was glad" (John 8:56). Is it possible that "partially hardened," God-fearing Jews receive a special grace because they are looking forward to Yeshua's second coming?

Romans 11:25-26 says that the Jewish people are "partially hardened until the fullness of the Gentiles comes in" and then "all of Israel will be saved." Perhaps this means that the Jewish people will remain partially hardened until the fullness of the Gentiles has come in. Therefore, attempts to evangelize the Jewish people before then will only cause harm.

Something very significant is happening in Israel right now. God is restoring His people and His land. According to the prophets, the Jewish people returning home, the land being restored, the Hebrew language being spoken on the streets, etc., are all precursors to the final redemption when Yeshua will come and reign from Zion. If the God-fearing Jewish people in Israel are in this redemptive "flow," if they are actively headed in that direction, then maybe they aren't the ones we should be concerned about. It seems that God has them exactly where He wants them to be.

Lastly, the God-fearing Jewish people have and are preserving many core identity markers of Yeshua's coming kingdom: Jerusalem as its capital, the Torah as its constitution, the people of Israel and those who join her as its citizens, Hebrew as its language, etc. Without the Jewish people's care, many—if not all —of these would have been lost! Maybe God will offer the Jewish people a special grace during their partially-hardened state because they have guarded, even unto death, these God-ordained elements that will be part of Yeshua's coming kingdom.

I recognize that I just plowed through a theological minefield. On one hand, these thoughts may feel off base because we know that no one can come to the Father except through Yeshua. It also seems wrong and grossly arrogant to say that these people, whom God partially hardened and is working through in our day, are all Hell-bound.

Here are my conclusions:

I should continue my walk with Yeshua, knowing that He has a master plan of salvation that includes redemption for the entire world—the nations and the Jewish people.

Loving God's Chosen People

I should repent of and no longer join "Amalek" in the generational fight against God's chosen people—even if they do not believe in Yeshua as Messiah.

It is above my pay grade to determine whether any person is destined for Hell. It would be very arrogant of me to say that the Jewish people, who have played a significant role in enabling me to find salvation, are eternally damned.

Because of the Amalek partnerships in Christian history and because I think God may have a merciful plan for those He "partially hardened," I believe it is good to have relationships with Orthodox Jews without any expectation of changing them. I think proselytizing is insensitive and actually increases the hatred of Yeshua in Israel.

One more question arises as we contemplate our end-times view of "the fullness of the Gentiles" and the salvation of "all Israel." We believe that Yeshua will return as a conquering king. All of His enemies will be put under His feet, and He will bring peace and righteousness to the entire world. When the Jewish people hear this, several memories flash before their eyes. They see a crusader king marching through Israel slaughtering men, women, and children with the slogan "kiss the cross or die!" What if this type of Christian leader arises, as many times in the past? Will all the Christians say that he is Yeshua and join him in purging Israel of all those who are against him?

I believe that when Yeshua comes, He will be the same "Lion of the tribe of Judah", "Son of Abraham", "Root of David", Torah-observant Jew that He was the first time He came. The difference will be that this time, He will fulfill the rest of what the Messiah is prophesied to do.

Because of this, He will be recognized as the Messiah by God-fearing Jewish people. They will "look on [Him] whom they pierced" and "all Israel will be saved." In other words, if the Jewish people do not see Him as the Messiah, then he is not the Messiah! The Jewish people's declaration that He is the Messiah will be a qualifier for all of us that it is indeed Yeshua, the Messiah.

To summarize, I would like to leave you with these thoughts. The Orthodox Zionist Jews are on the front lines, fighting in defense of God's chosen land, people, and Word. In order to turn this bus around and head to the Mount of Blessing, are we willing to join with the Jewish people and conquer anti-Zionism, anti-Semitism, and anti-Judaism?

CHAPTER SEVENTEEN

Modern Israel - Man's Creation or God's Hand?

Zac Waller

As I have traveled around the world sharing about the miracle of Israel's rebirth, I have encountered well-meaning Christians who claim that the modern State of Israel is secular, pagan, and against the will of God. They point to the fact that many of the founders of modern Israel were atheist, that the government is secular and not Torah-based, and that many Jewish Israelis returned to Israel because they felt they would have a better chance of security and success, not because of any biblical motivation.

So the question is raised: Is the modern State of Israel the work of mere men seeking survival, or is it the hand of God fulfilling His word to restore the land and people of Israel?

The word of God has a lot to say about how the restoration of Israel will take place. In the book of Deuteronomy chapter thirty, Moses prophesies that the children of Israel would go into exile. He says that they would remember the blessings and the curses and return to the Lord. It speaks of how they would be gathered back to the land, flourish in it, and that God would circumcise their hearts and cause them to walk in His ways. Verse ten repeats the statement that they would "return" to the Lord.

A careful look at the text provokes a question. In order to be restored, Israel has to bring to mind all of the blessings and curses, and then she has to return to HaShem and obey His voice. After receiving mercy, being gathered back, and becoming prosperous, God says He will "circumcise your heart." If Israel has already "returned to HaShem," why do they need their hearts to be circumcised?

It seems that there is an initial turning, and then a cleaning up after the return home. What's more, is that in most of our English translations, verses two and ten both say "return to the Lord." In the original Hebrew text, there are two different words used for "to." The word used in verse two means "until," or "up to," while the word in verse ten means "to," "towards," or "into."

The difference in these two words also confirms that the initial turning that Israel will experience is not a full return. Much of the process of repentance and turning from evil back to God happens after the children of Israel have returned home.

Let's take a look at another prophecy about the ingathering of the exiles. Ezekiel 36:24-25 says: "For I will take you from among the nations, gather you out of all countries, and bring you into your own land. Then I will sprinkle clean water on you, and you shall be clean; I will cleanse you from all your filthiness and from all your idols."

God says that they could even be worshipping idols when they come back! Does He leave them that way? No! He cleans them up after He brings them home!

These biblical examples clearly show that Israel will not be perfect and fully following God before the "greater exodus." But, if this is true, we should see some indications that as the Jewish people are coming back they are continuing their "turning" process.

Let's take a look at a few quotes from the founders of the modern state of Israel. David Ben Gurion, Israel's first prime minister, stated in the declaration of independence:

"The Land of Israel was the birthplace of the Jewish people. Here their spiritual, religious, and political identity was shaped. Here they first attained to statehood, created cultural values of national and universal significance, and gave to the world the eternal Book of Books. After being forcibly exiled from their land, the people kept faith with it throughout their Dispersion and never ceased to pray and hope for their return to it and for the restoration in it of their political freedom.

Impelled by this historic and traditional attachment, Jews strove in every successive generation to re-establish themselves in their ancient homeland."

"The State of Israel will be open for Jewish immigration and for the Ingathering of the Exiles."

"Placing our trust in the Rock of Israel, we affix our signatures to this proclamation."

It is important to note that this is the declaration of independence - a public document declaring to the world the intent of establishing this new state! You cannot help but notice the very strong biblical motivation for creating the State of Israel!

Prime Minister Ben Gurion appointed Rabbi Shlomo (Solomon) Goren as the first Chief Rabbi of the IDF. Rabbi Shlomo Goren

Footnote: https://www.knesset.gov.il/docs/eng/megilat_eng.htm

Modern Israel - Man's Creation or God's Hand?

was known as a brilliant Torah scholar who had also served in the newly formed Jewish army. This begs the question, if the Prime Minister's intentions were completely secular, why would he appoint a very observant, God-fearing leader to make decisions about its newly formed, fledgling army?

During Israel's fight for survival, Rabbi Shlomo Goren was known for walking right into the thick of battle carrying a Torah Scroll and a shofar (as depicted in the pictures when he went in with the troops to liberate Jerusalem's Old City). He would often quote Psalms 91:7-11 "A thousand may fall at your side, and ten thousand at your right hand; but it shall not come near you. Only with your eyes shall you look, and see the reward of the wicked. Because you have made the Lord, who is my refuge, even the Most High, your dwelling place, no evil shall befall you, nor shall any plague come near your dwelling; for He shall give His angels charge over you, to keep you in all your ways." He would then walk into the most dangerous battle fronts, returning unscathed. He put his trust in the God of Israel, and God honored him for it.

Rabbi Goren did his best to make sure his soldiers had kosher food to eat, time and places to pray, and he produced a tiny book of Psalms that the soldiers could take with them into battle. He knew that the IDF needed to be spiritually strong in order for God to bless them with success in battle. It's no secret that God

Footnote: Goren, Rabbi Shlomo, *With Might and Strength,* (New Milford: Maggid Books, 2016).

has blessed the IDF over and over again, against all odds, with victory over their enemies.

Probably the most significant point is that we are seeing things happen in today's time that are unprecedented and impossible without divine assistance!

The Hebrew language was not spoken "on the street" for 2,000 years. It is an absolute miracle that the nation of Israel is speaking it today. The prophet Zephaniah prophesied that this would happen!

The Jewish people were scattered out to the four corners of the earth, exactly as prophesied. Now they are returning in huge numbers to their ancient homeland! This has not happened since the Romans exiled the Jews from Israel. It is miraculous that they have maintained their identity while in exile, and it is miraculous that they are returning, exactly as prophesied!

The land of Israel lay desolate for 2,000 years. Today it is flourishing with trees, vines, and produce, exactly as prophesied.

The Torah has not been observed on a national level in 2,000 years. Today there is a chief Rabbi of Israel working to enable Israel to follow the Torah. Many Jewish people are embracing their biblical roots and responding to God's hand as He turns them towards Him.

There has not been an Israeli army since the Maccabees. For an army of refugees to gather right after the holocaust from many nations and languages to defeat enemies that greatly outnumbered them was a miracle! And yes, the prophets also said that would happen!

Yes, there are Jewish Israelis who God has not turned all the way around yet. But to say that these incredibly significant events that lay dormant for two thousand years—that are taking place in our day exactly as prophesied—are all happenstance, is in my opinion, a very dangerous claim.

I believe it is time for us as Christians to begin treating the Jewish people with the love and respect that is fitting for God's anointed, chosen people. They are our brothers and our partners with God in bringing about the final redemption. Let's recognize this "hour of visitation" and partner with God as He restores the Land and people of Israel!

CHAPTER EIGHTEEN

Never Divide the Land of Israel

Luke Hilton

World leaders are constantly striving for peace, alliances, and the elimination of conflict. Businesses used to run competitively (and some still do), but there's a growing culture in which everyone must have equal chances, regardless of their performance. Children in the public school system are largely treated the same, regardless of their work or grade point average. Children in sports are told that it's not about being competitive, but about everyone having a good time.

People are afraid to choose sides. Christians especially so, I think, because their faith already puts them in a box, and they're afraid of distancing themselves even further from those around them. Those who are ready to stand firmly on biblical principles seem to be dwindling in numbers. If we want to truly walk as our Messiah walked, though, this path will never work.

There are lots of areas I could address while on this topic, but I want to narrow in on only one. It's the Israel issue.

For some reason, Israel is on the agenda of nearly every government in the world. American presidents for decades have had the issue of peace in the Middle East at the top of their agenda when coming into power. However, no one has been able to solve the issue. No one has succeeded in creating peace in the land that God gave to Abraham, Isaac, and Jacob so many thousands of years ago.

I can say with the utmost confidence that the reason none of these plans have succeeded is that each and every leader missed one crucial piece to the puzzle. Many of these US presidents were evangelical Christians—some Catholics, some Democrats, and some Republicans. None of them, however, used the Scriptures as the foundation for their peace plans. If they had, I have a feeling they would have found much greater success in their endeavors.

If so many world leaders have failed to create peace in the Middle East, what does that mean for us? First of all, we need to consult the Bible.

Zechariah 14 talks about a day when all nations will come to fight against Jerusalem. It doesn't say might or if. It says God *will* gather all nations to battle against Jerusalem. It's part of His grand master plan.

However, there are consequences for those nations who join in fighting against Israel.

"Then the LORD will go forth and fight against those nations, as He fights on the day of battle. And on that day His feet will stand on the Mount of Olives, which faces Jerusalem on the east" (Zechariah 14:3-4b).

I, for one, do not want the LORD fighting against me. Even though all nations will one day come against Israel, that doesn't mean we do not have an individual responsibility. In a time when the world is falling prey to complacency and passiveness, this is an especially important issue that we cannot afford to be on the fence about.

We already spoke about President Trump's peace plan for Israel, commonly known as the "deal of the century." When the plan first came out, nearly the entire conservative world, both Christians and Jews, were advocating for its implementation. It calls for Israel to apply sovereignty over thirty percent of the West Bank, something that no US president has ever dared to try before. As previously noted, the plan also contains hidden dangers that would mean near suicide for Israel.

One of the huge dangers that the plan promotes is the establishment of a Palestinian state to be governed by the Palestinian Authority. Remember that in no uncertain terms, the PA supports, promotes, and teaches its people to murder and terrorize Jews. It teaches violence in its public school systems from a young age, advocates for jihad in its mosques, and pays significant monthly salaries to those who manage to kill or maim Jews and are sent to Israeli prisons! It actively participates in blatant Jew hatred and Jew killing! I know that this is strong language, but it is one hundred percent true. I've talked to Palestinians personally and heard these facts for myself.

The "deal of the century" also calls for fifteen of the settlements in Judea and Samaria to exist only as enclaves, surrounded by a Palestinian state. Remember, we are talking about a most certainly terrorist state. How would you like to have a terrorist state on your country's borders?

Part of the plan that only came out after Israel had accepted it also states that a complete building freeze would be enacted on the settlements, not only forbidding expansion but also disallowing the Israelis to build vertically on existing buildings.

Make no mistake about it: as good as the plan is, President Trump's "deal of the century" undoubtedly calls for the division of the land of Israel. As we've already said, Joel 3 outlines very disastrous consequences for such a move.

Never Divide the Land of Israel

Every peace plan that has preceded the "deal of the century" has failed. None of them were founded on the Word of God. None of them looked at what the prophets of the Bible had to say about their formulations. All of them experienced disastrous consequences for their nation.

So what is God's peace plan? Instead of trying to explain it, here's what the prophets have to say:

"And it shall come to pass that everyone who is left of all the nations which came against Jerusalem shall go up from year to year to worship the King, the LORD of hosts, and to keep the Feast of Tabernacles" (Zechariah 14:16).

"For I know the thoughts that I think toward you, says the LORD, thoughts of peace and not of evil, to give you a future and a hope. Then you will call upon Me and go and pray to Me, and I will listen to you. And you will seek Me and find Me, when you search for Me with all your heart. I will be found by you, says the LORD, and I will bring you back from your captivity; I will gather you from all the nationals and from all the places where I have driven you, says the LORD, and I will bring you to the place from which I cause you to be carried away captive" (Jeremiah 29:11-14).

"Also the sons of the foreigner who join themselves to the LORD, to serve Him, and to love the name of the LORD, to be His servants - everyone who keeps from defiling the sabbath, and holds fast My covenant—even them I will bring to My holy mountain, and make them joyful in My house of prayer. Their burn offerings and their sacrifices will be accepted on My altar; for My house shall be called a house of prayer for all nations" (Isaiah 56:6-7).

"Now it shall come to pass in the latter days that the mountain of the LORD's house shall be established on the top of the mountains, and shall be exalted above the hills and all nations shall flow to it. Many people shall come and say 'come and let us go up to the mountain of the LORD, to the house of the God of Jacob; He will teach us His ways, and we shall walk in His paths.' For out of Zion shall go forth the law, and the word of the LORD from Jerusalem. He shall judge between the nations, and rebuke many people; they shall beat their swords into plowshares, and their spears into pruning hooks; nation shall not lift up sword against nation, neither shall they learn war anymore" (Isaiah 2:2-4).

CHAPTER NINETEEN

Lightly Esteeming Israel

Luke Hilton

Most Christians are familiar with the blessing of Abraham. Genesis 12:3 has become an iconic verse for many pro-Israel Christians, Zionists, Messianics, and Hebrew Roots followers. It's been so well used, it has even reached the point of abuse in some circles, with organizations using the verse to raise money as they promise wealth and prosperity for those who donate to help Israel. In this chapter, I want to dig deeper into what the blessing of Abraham really is and its place in Christianity.

"I will bless those who bless you, and curse those who curse you, and in you, all the families of the earth shall be blessed" (Genesis 12:3).

This verse is the first record of God's promise to Abraham, and directly after it, we find that Abraham traveled to a place called Elon Moreh, where, as he gazed out over the Tirzah Valley toward the Mount of Blessing and the Mount of Cursing and the valley of Shechem, God told him, " … to you and your descendants I will give this land" (Genesis 12:7). On a side note, this is a great visual teaser to encourage you to come and visit the biblical Heartland, stand where Abraham stood, and see your Bible come to life! The Tirzah Valley, ironically, is the route that the children of Israel took to enter the land with Joshua many years later.

We won't go through all of the passages recording the blessing of Abraham, but numerous times throughout Genesis, we see God promising the same thing to him, then passing it down to Isaac and to Jacob. The theme of the story stays the same:

- I will bless those who bless you.

- I will give you a land and make you a great nation.

- In you, all families of the earth shall be blessed.

Did you know that there are two different Hebrew words for curse in Genesis 12? The first word for curse means exactly what you would think—not a pretty definition. The second word for curse is actually a different Hebrew term meaning "to lightly esteem." If we re-translate this verse using the definitions for the Hebrew words for curse, this is how Genesis 12:3 would read:

"I will bless those who bless you and curse those who lightly esteem you."

Ouch! God did not take this blessing to Abraham lightly. Four thousand years ago, when God laid out the plan for redeeming and blessing a fallen world, He laid out the terms very clearly. Not only did He choose a special people and nation, but He also planned for the rest of the world to walk in blessing through those special people.

He even went as far as to say that if we lightly esteem Abraham's descendants, we will be cursed. Kinda changes our perspective on the blessing of Abraham, doesn't it?

Some choose to take this story and go down the path of anti-Semitism. Sadly, we've seen a horrific history between Christians and Jews for the last 2,000 years as millions of Jews have been persecuted and even lost their lives due to this evil lie. Instead of joining in the promise of Abraham, many nations choose to hate the blessing.

Others choose the lie of replacement theology, a false doctrine that states that God did away with Israel and replaced them with the Church. This is a very dangerous position and has also contributed to the last 2,000 years of separation between Christianity and Judaism.

Still others choose to join in with the blessing of Abraham (and we have seen a rise in this position in the last few decades). This leads me to my main point: one of the key themes in the Abrahamic story is that God promised him that all families of the earth would be blessed through him! God is not just speaking of the fact that if we bless Israel we will be blessed. He's talking about physical, spiritual, mental, and emotional wellbeing. God promised to bless all families of the earth through Abraham and his descendants. That's an incredible opportunity!

Instead of trying to explain away the blessing, replace it, or fight against it, we can choose to join in, realizing that our very lives are intertwined with this story! Over the centuries, many people have held onto resentment towards the blessing of Abraham, which many times led to terrible persecution. Instead, we have the opportunity to walk with our brothers and sisters, realizing that this is the place where blessing for the nations comes from.

"Now it shall come to pass in the latter days that the mountain of the LORD's house shall be established on the top of the mountains and shall be exalted above the hills; and peoples shall flow to it. Many nations shall come and say, 'Come, and let us go up to the mountain of the LORD, to the house of the God of Jacob; He will teach us His ways, and we shall walk in His paths.' For out of Zion the law shall go forth, and the word of the LORD from Jerusalem" (Micah 4:1-3).

God's Word will go forth from Jerusalem! One day, many nations will want to go up to the mountain of the LORD, to His house. This goes hand in hand with Isaiah 56:7, which states:

"Even them (speaking of the foreigner) I will bring to My holy mountain, and make them joyful in My house of prayer; for My house shall be called a house of prayer for all nations."

God didn't exclusively bless Abraham and his descendants so that the rest of the world would be condemned or live outside of His blessing. He crafted a beautiful plan in which all nations and families would be abundantly blessed through a man called Abraham. This plan includes you, me, and anyone who chooses to stand on God's promises.

We could spend pages more describing the opportunities that the prophets gave for the nations to be involved in this special story. I'll leave you with just one:

"How beautiful upon the mountains are the feet of him who brings good news, who proclaims peace, who brings glad tidings of good things, who proclaims salvation, who says to Zion, 'Your God reigns!'" (Isaiah 52:7).

Our organization, HaYovel, brings beautiful feet to Judea and Samaria, the Biblical Heartland of Israel, where we choose to take part in the beautiful promise of Abraham and participate in all of the wonderful blessings that the prophets foretold. We'd like to invite you to participate in this beautiful prophecy. Whether or not you join our organization, we encourage you to come to Israel's Heartland and join in the restoration of God's kingdom.

God's promise to Abraham is forever. And I do mean forever.

CHAPTER TWENTY

The Sun & Moon Predictions

Zac Waller

"Everlasting", "perpetual", "throughout your generations", "from generation to generation", "to a thousand generations", "forevermore"— the Bible is replete with these words and phrases.

God loves communicating eternal precepts through His Word to His people. He is "the same today and yesterday and forever" (Hebrews 13:8). He is the Lord, and He does not change (Malachi 3:6).

By revealing things that never change, God shows His own eternal nature, His faithfulness, His trustworthiness and His ability to foreknow the needs of humanity.

All throughout Psalms, it is proclaimed that God's steadfast love endures forever. What an amazing statement! The Almighty God, Creator of the universe, has steadfast, unfailing, never-ending love for you and me! This love did not stop when you were born or when you made your first mistake. It didn't stop when you committed the worst sin of your life. God's love is always there. He desires you and will never turn you down when you turn to Him.

What other things does God consider so important that He would declare it to be "forever"?

His covenants!

In Genesis 9, God makes a covenant with Noah: "I establish my covenant with you, that never again shall all flesh be cut off by the waters of the flood, and never again shall there be a flood to destroy the earth."

Though the world has seen much evil since Noah's day, God has been faithful to His covenant.

Six chapters later, in Genesis 15, we see God making a covenant with Abraham:
"On that day the LORD made a covenant with Abram, saying, "To your offspring I give this land, from the river of Egypt to the great river, the river Euphrates, the land of the Kenites, the Kenizzites, the Kadmonites, the Hittites, the Perizzites, the

Rephaim, the Amorites, the Canaanites, the Girgashites and the Jebusites."

Many Christians have come to the conclusion that this covenant was somehow nullified, that God only chose Abraham, his descendants, and the land of Israel for a certain amount of time. After that, God was done with them and moved on to Plan B. Is this biblically sound? Let's take a look at several other Scriptures.

"He is the Lord our God; his judgments are in all the earth. He remembers his covenant forever, the word that he commanded, for a thousand generations, the covenant that he made with Abraham, his sworn promise to Isaac, which he confirmed to Jacob as a statute, to Israel as an everlasting covenant, saying, 'To you I will give the land of Canaan as your portion for an inheritance'" (Psalm 150:7-11).

"Thus says the Lord, who gives the sun for a light by day, the ordinances of the moon and the stars for a light by night, who disturbs the sea, and its waves roar (The Lord of hosts is His name): 'If those ordinances depart from before Me, says the Lord, then the seed of Israel shall also cease from being a nation before Me forever'"(Jeremiah 31:35-36).

"I will not violate my covenant or alter the word that went forth from my lips. Once for all I have sworn by my holiness; I will not lie to David. His offspring shall endure forever, his throne as long as the sun before me. Like the moon it shall be established forever, a faithful witness in the skies" (Psalm 89:34-37).

As long as the sun rises in the morning and sets in the evening, we can count on God keeping His covenants! "But," some may say, "the people of Israel were not faithful to God, so He had to let them go." The Scriptures actually refute this false idea, as well.

Deuteronomy 29 contains devastating prophecies about Israel's falling away from God. Moses tells the people that they will be exiled, and their land will become desolate, and then "all the nations will say, 'Why has the Lord done thus to this land? What caused the heat of this great anger?' Then people will say, 'It is because they abandoned the covenant of the Lord, the God of their fathers, which he made with them when he brought them out of the land of Egypt.'"

Most Christians would end there, but Moses did not! He continues in Chapter 30:

"And when all these things come upon you, the blessing and the curse, which I have set before you, and you call them to mind among all the nations where the Lord your God has driven you, and return to the Lord your God, you and your children, and obey his voice in all that I command you today, with all your heart and with all your soul, then the Lord your God will restore your fortunes and have mercy on you, and he will gather you again from all the peoples where the Lord your God has scattered you."

Throughout the Prophets, we see the same narrative: Israel will sin, Israel will be punished severely, it will seem as though God has forgotten Israel, and then God will redeem the people of Israel and bring them back to their land.

Also, if we back up a few verses in our passage from Psalm 89, we read: "My steadfast love I will keep for him forever, and my covenant will stand firm for him. I will establish his offspring forever and his throne as the days of the heavens. If his children forsake my law and do not walk according to my rules, if they violate my statutes and do not keep my commandments, then I will punish their transgression with the rod and their iniquity with stripes, but I will not remove from him my steadfast love or be false to my faithfulness. I will not violate my covenant or alter the word that went forth from my lips."

God's covenant-keeping faithfulness does not depend on Israel's ability to keep their end of the deal. God's Word declares that Israel will be restored! The people and land of Israel are destined for full redemption.

Many Christians will reason that God's covenant with the Jews ended when Yeshua came and enacted the new covenant. This is a very misguided view of covenants! Was God's covenant with Noah also annulled when Yeshua came?

There is not a stage one and two of forever! "Everlasting" is not a two-part plan! God's plan was good from the beginning. Yeshua came to further establish the will of His Father. As I stated earlier in the book, Yeshua was in it from the beginning. These covenants are His plan. If we oppose them, we oppose Him!

Let's take a look at one last covenant: the Davidic covenant. In 2 Samuel 7, God speaks to King David through Nathan the prophet, saying:

"When your days are fulfilled and you lie down with your fathers, I will raise up your offspring after you, who shall come from your body, and I will establish his kingdom. He shall build a house for my name, and I will establish the throne of his kingdom forever. I will be to him a father, and he shall be to me a son. When he commits iniquity, I will discipline him with the rod of men, with the stripes of the sons of men, but my steadfast love will not depart from him, as I took it from Saul, whom I put away from before you. And your house and your kingdom shall be made sure forever before me. Your throne shall be established forever."

Exactly as prophesied, King David's son Solomon became king and built a house for God. It is interesting to note that at the dedication of the house, King Solomon prays this prayer:

"... When a foreigner, who is not of your people Israel, comes from a far country for the sake of your great name and your mighty hand and your outstretched arm, when he comes and prays toward this house, hear from heaven your dwelling place and do according to all for which the foreigner calls to you, in order that all the peoples of the earth may know your name and fear you, as do your people Israel, and that they may know that this house that I have built is called by your name"(2 Chron. 14:32-33).

Almost 1,000 years later, another Son of David and King of Israel, Yeshua, the Messiah of Israel, stood in the courtyard of the Temple. Merchants had set up their wares in the very spot that was dedicated for foreigners to come and pray. Yeshua passionately and almost violently pushed the merchants outside the Temple compound while quoting the words of Isaiah the prophet: "My house shall be called a house of prayer for all nations"!

Perhaps King Solomon and King Yeshua give us some insight into the purpose of these God-breathed covenants. Perhaps they are part of God's master plan of salvation for the entire world. Why would Solomon be thinking about the other nations of the world when he was dedicating the Temple of God in Jerusalem? Why would Yeshua have quoted this verse as He stood in the courtyard of His Father's house? They were very aware of God's heart as they stood in His house. God wants world revival, and He has a plan to accomplish that great task. His covenants are a very significant part of that plan!

If that is true, then those of us who call on His name should rally behind Him! We should be the first ones speaking words and taking actions to affirm these redemption-thrusting covenants that the Almighty made with Israel and the Jewish people. It's time to move!

CHAPTER TWENTY-ONE

The Promise for the Foreigner

Luke Hilton

Back to the foreigners. I know what you're thinking: "I don't want to be a foreigner! Besides, Ephesians says that we are part of the commonwealth of Israel and no longer strangers to the covenants of promise!"

I totally agree. Through Yeshua our Messiah, we have a place in the covenant that God made with Abraham, Isaac, and Jacob. We are part of His family.

However, most of us reading this are still part of the nations (unless you're Jewish). If you showed up in Israel, you would not fit in with the nation of Israel.

Do you know what's amazing? Being known as the "nations" is not a bad thing! Yes, it is true that there are many negative prophecies concerning the nations, but there are also beautiful, positive prophecies for the nations—especially when they align themselves with the God of Israel. At the end of days, the Messianic Kingdom will be made up of the Messiah ruling over all nations from Jerusalem. At that time, there will be two categories of peoples: those from Israel and those from the nations. And all nations will come up to worship God in Jerusalem during the Feast of Tabernacles (Zechariah 14). That is an exciting prophecy and something to look forward to! Do you believe that God has an everlasting covenant with His land and people Israel that will never become null and void? Do you believe that Yeshua (Yeshua) bestowed salvation on you and brought you into that covenant that He made with Abraham?

Do you believe that the entire Bible, from Genesis to Revelation is one hundred percent true and applicable to us today? If you answered yes to those questions, it might be time for a realignment in your life. When Solomon built the Temple and dedicated it, he specifically prayed for the foreigner. He begged God that, in the generations following, whenever people from other nations stretched out their hands and prayed toward the Temple in Jerusalem, God in Heaven would hear and answer their prayer.

The Promise for the Foreigner

We're living in a time when each day is unexpected. World pandemics, riots, protests, violence, and hate abound. At the same time, we're seeing an interest in the Bible we've never seen before. Pastors and Christian leaders are bringing God's people together for prayer and unity in an expectation that God will begin to move among His people once again.

What if the only missing ingredient to this world revival is a turning to Jerusalem? We've clearly seen in the chapters in this book that all throughout history, God had a plan to choose a special people and place to put His name. After that people and place were chosen, history shows us that Israel never lost their connection to Jerusalem. The Temple was destroyed and rebuilt twice. Currently, the Jewish people are doing everything they can to see the Temple rebuilt for the third and final time! Unprecedented numbers of Jews and Christians are ascending to the Temple Mount, the same place that Yeshua declared should be a house of prayer for all nations.

It is clear that our Messiah loved Jerusalem and the Temple, even from a young age. We find recorded all throughout the Gospels that He was constantly in Jerusalem, teaching in the Temple. He was an Orthodox Jewish Rabbi Who could constantly be found traveling to Jerusalem, many times for the biblical festivals.

When Yeshua was not in Jerusalem, He was always found in the synagogue on Shabbat, as was His custom. The synagogue could be likened to a mini-Temple, and was (and still is) built so that its congregants face Jerusalem. Even the synagogue leaders don't face their congregation during prayer times, but rather face Jerusalem along with the congregants.

I truly believe that the church was meant to be built the same as the synagogue. The Christian faith was never meant to be so separated from its first-century brother, Judaism. Even the early disciples were Orthodox Jewish men and women!

We find all throughout the Gospels that the Jewish believers participated in the feasts, daily prayers, and practices in the synagogues—and in the Temple! We even find Paul participating in the custom of the Nazirite vow in the Temple in Jerusalem. When the Holy Spirit was poured out at Pentecost, the disciples were in Jerusalem, almost for certain in the Temple courts. We read in Acts 2 that they were in one accord in one place, another term for the Temple. The Holy Spirit was poured out on them after they were (1) in one accord, (2) in the same place (the Temple), and (3) spent all night in prayer.

If Christianity today would lay down the theological blockade of 40,000+ denominations and duplicate the model of that first Pentecost, I am confident that we would see a similar outpouring of the Holy Spirit.

The Promise for the Foreigner

Many people quote the famous passage in 2 Chronicles 7:14, asking God to heal their land. Unfortunately, most people disconnect that passage completely from its original intent. God was speaking about the land of Israel! However, I do believe that if nations were to turn towards Jerusalem, unite in prayer, and ask God to heal their land, He would do it.

I am one hundred percent sure that the missing key to world revival is Jerusalem. All throughout Scripture, we see this important part of our faith, which has unfortunately been removed from Christian doctrine. Not only the entire Bible, but our Messiah and the first-century church were intrinsically connected to Jerusalem and the Temple. Yeshua and His disciples would have faced Jerusalem and said the *Shema* ("Hear O Israel, the LORD our God is One") every day! If our Messiah and His disciples were so connected with Jerusalem, then so should we be. Yeshua even said that the *Shema* was the greatest commandment!

It's time to align ourselves with the God of Abraham, Isaac, and Jacob, all of Scripture, and Yeshua our Messiah.
It's time to align ourselves with Zion.

CHAPTER TWENTY-TWO

Time for Action

Zac Waller

After reading through the chapters of this book, my hope is that you have been inspired to take action. In this final chapter, I would like to share a few action points that have been beneficial in our journey. My goal is to support you as you continue on your journey toward being aligned with God, becoming like Yeshua, and building God's kingdom on Earth as it is in Heaven.

Daniel in the lion's den is one of the most well-known Bible stories. Did you know that it specifically says that, when Daniel prayed in Babylon, he turned to face Jerusalem? Daniel was thrown into the lion's den for praying to the God of Israel!

It is time for us to align ourselves with Zion! At night, before heading to bed, I gather my family together, and we face towards Jerusalem to pray. The *Shema* is a very special prayer and one that we include in our daily prayer times. It is taken from Deuteronomy 6:4: "Hear, O Israel: The Lord our God, the Lord is one!" In Hebrew, it reads: "*Shema Yisrael, Adonai Eloheinu, Adonai echad.*"

This verse has many deep meanings. Two main concepts are that (1) we are acknowledging that we are praying to the God of Israel and (2) He is one, not many different gods.

It is a very special Scripture to us Christians because Yeshua mentions it as the greatest commandment in Mark 12:28-30:

"... One of the scribes came, and having heard them reasoning together, perceiving that He had answered them well, asked Him, 'Which is the first commandment of all?' Yeshua answered him, 'The first of all the commandments is: 'Hear, O Israel, the Lord our God, the Lord is one. And you shall love the Lord your God with all your heart, with all your soul, with all your mind, and with all your strength.' This is the first commandment.'"

As we face towards Jerusalem, my family and I also pray Yeshua's prayer, the "Our Father," from Matthew 6:8-13:

"Our Father in heaven, Hallowed be Your name. Your kingdom come. Your will be done On earth as it is in heaven. Give us this day our daily bread. And forgive us our debts, As we forgive our debtors. And do not lead us into temptation, But deliver us from the evil one. For Yours is the kingdom and the power and the glory forever. Amen."

As we pray "on Earth as it is in Heaven," I can't help but think of how God's glory was in the Temple in Jerusalem and of how Yeshua is coming soon to reign from Zion!

As you pray, don't forget the biblical mandate to "pray for the peace of Jerusalem" (Psalm 122:6). God will grow the yearning in your heart to be with Him as you face towards His house and seek His kingdom.

You have probably heard of Corrie ten Boom and her book *The Hiding Place*. She has an amazing testimony of saving many Jews during World War II. She was sent to a concentration camp and barely made it out alive due to a clerical error.

What many do not know about her story is that her grandfather, Willem ten Boom, saw the Scripture to pray for the peace of Jerusalem and started a prayer meeting every week to pray for Israel and the Jewish people. Remember, this was before the rebirth of the state of Israel! What a man of faith! We see the incredible fruit of his prayers lived out in the lives of his son, grandchildren, and great-grandchildren during World War II.

The next action item I would recommend is to study the Scriptures. Read the Prophets and highlight the things that are being fulfilled right now. Pray that the things that are not yet fulfilled would be fulfilled soon and in our days!

Study the words of Yeshua and the apostles in the context of a Gospel that includes God's established people, place, times, and communication. Yeshua is the Living Word. That is the same Word that God gave to Moses!

I encourage you to be intentional about connecting with Israel. There are so many ministries that are pumping out great content. In this age of technology, email, podcasts, and YouTube videos, it is very easy to stay up-to-date and involved in what God is doing in Israel.

Find ways to invest in Israel. Matthew 6:21 says, "... Where your treasure is, there your heart will be also." The work of God is going full steam in Israel! It is bringing much glory to His name! By investing in Israel, we partner with God as He fulfills His word to restore His land and people.

Come to the land! You will never be the same after experiencing the land where the Bible was written. Your Bible will come alive, and your faith will be strengthened. You will gain more of an understanding of what God is doing here and be able to better discuss these things in your sphere of influence.

Time for Action

God says in Isaiah 56 that He will take all the people from outside Israel who love and serve Him and bring them to Jerusalem and make them joyful in His house of prayer. God wants you to come visit and talk to Him at His house!

Lastly, please take a stand against those who seek to divide God's land. If that means having a conversation at your local grocery store or contacting your senators and congressmen, please do whatever you can! As Edmond Burke put it, "The only thing necessary for the triumph of evil is for good men to do nothing."

For Zion's sake, let's take our place as watchmen on the walls of Jerusalem, aligning ourselves with the God, people, and land of Israel to build the Kingdom of God on Earth as it is in Heaven!

ACTION QUESTIONS:

1. How will you pray towards Zion for the peace of Jerusalem?

2. What topics or books in the Bible are you committed to studying?

3. Where is your treasure/heart? How will you sow into Israel?

4. When are you going to come to Israel?

5. How will you speak up for Israel?

ACKNOWLEDGEMENTS

Many people were a part of this project, and we couldn't have done it without them. It's impossible to thank everyone, but we'd like to give it our best shot.

Our parents, Tommy and Sherri Waller and Randy and Lynne Hilton, for instilling in us a vision and passion for the restoration of God's Kingdom in Jerusalem.

Our wives, Olivia Hilton and Becca Waller, for their outpouring of love and support as we continue to walk out our personal calling in our lives.

The editors - besides the professional editing, we were blessed to have a number of in house editors who gave their valuable feedback - Lynne Hilton, Katelyn Waller & Katie Waller.

For all of those who read the book before its release and offered feedback - Michael Card, Earl Cox, Dean Bye, Sharon Sanders, Pastor Trey Graham, Ben Hilton, Sherri Waller, Lynne Hilton, Drew Parson, and Steve Hoelscher.

We'd like to thank our friends in Israel for allowing us to come to Israel, make reparation for Christianity's negative past, and learn and grow in our understanding of the bible.

Lastly, but most importantly, we'd like to thank the God of Abraham, Isaac and Jacob for allowing us to be a part of His Kingdom, and allowing us to be vessels for conveying the message of the Kingdom to the world. We would not be here without His redeeming grace.

Printed in Great Britain
by Amazon